Library of
Davidson College

The Art and Craft of Poetry

by
Daisy Aldan

North River Press

© Copyright 1981 by Daisy Aldan. All Rights Reserved. No part of this work may be reproduced, except for brief excerpts for review purposes, without written permission of the publisher.

Manufactured in the United States of America

Library of Congress Cataloging in Publication Data

Aldan, Daisy.
    The art and craft of poetry.

    1. Poetics.   I. Title.
PN1042.A48   808.1   80-27694
ISBN 0-88427-047-5

Contents

Foreword	1
How May the Poet Develop Himself as an Artist?	3
The Journal	4
Expository and Aesthetic Writing	5
Elements of the Poet's Concern	7
Intention	11
Stream of Consciousness	18
Meditated Stream of Consciousness	20
Imagery	22

Some Uses of Imagery–23; Objective and Subjective Imagery–24; Some Characteristics of Imagery and Symbol–25; The Image and the Symbol–23; Figures of Speech–30; Imagery of Waking Consciousness, Memory, and Dream–36

The Appeal to the Senses	43

Hearing–44; Sight–48; Smell–52; Taste–54; Touch–54

Tone	57
Sound Structure	66
Rhyme	71
Structure	77
Spacing	81
Stanza Forms	85

Stanza Forms with Defined Patterns–85; Some Classical Forms–88; Three Basic Forms of Poetry–96; Some Contemporary Forms of Poetry–101

Metre and Rhythm	108

Evaluating the Poem	115
Preparing for Publication	117
The Poem *by Daisy Aldan*	120
Index to Authors and Poems	121

ACKNOWLEDGEMENTS

The poems of Daisy Aldan have appeared in *The Destruction of Cathedrals, Between High Tides, Or Learn to Walk on Water,* and *Breakthrough,* all copyright by Folder Editions, New York, N.Y. Reprinted by permission.

The poems of John Ashbery, Edward Field, Pauline Hanson, Frank O'Hara, and Sylvia Spenser have appeared in *Folder* Magazine and *A New Folder: Americans: Poems and Drawings,* edited and copyrighted by Daisy Aldan. Reprinted by permission.

"Living Space," by Roberta Gould is from *Writing Air, Written Water* (Waterside Press, New York, N.Y.). Copyright by Roberta Gould. Reprinted by permission.

"Aphrodite, her birth" by Alexandra Grilikhes is from *Isabel Rawsthorne Standing in A Street in Soho* (Folder Editions, New York, N.Y.). Copyright by Alexandra Grilikhes. Reprinted by permission.

"I come from the dreary city" by Albert Steffen is from *Selected Poems of Albert Steffen,* tr. by Daisy Aldan. Copyright by Folder Editions, New York, N.Y. Reprinted by permission.

"The Ghosts of Jersey City" by Lillian Morrison is from the book of the same title (T.Y. Crowell, New York, N.Y.). Copyright 1967 by Lillian Morrison. Reprinted by permission.

"In the Rif Mountains" by William Meredith will appear in *Shenandoah.* Copyright 1980 by *Shenandoah.* Reprinted by permission of the author.

"Seduction" by Phylis Goldberg. Copyright by the author. Reprinted by permission.

"From the Sea" by Susan Barrett is from *Ms. Noah Touches Earth* (Artichoke Press, Rancho Palos Verdes, Cal.). Copyright by Susan Barrett. Reprinted by permission.

"Translations from the Russian" is from *Suddenly Thunder* by Ruth Lisa Schechter (Barlenmir House, New York, N.Y.). Copyright by Ruth Lisa Schechter. Reprinted by permission.

"Rhadadevi's Dance" by Nayacandra Suri, "By The Seashore" by Rabindranath Tagore, and "The True and Tender Wife" by Valmiki are from *Poems of India,* Daisy Aldan, ed. (T.Y. Crowell Co., New York, N.Y.). Copyright by Daisy Aldan. Reprinted by permission.

"Fear" and "Relic" by Harriet Zinnes are from *An Eye for An I* (Folder Editions, New York, N.Y.). Copyright by Harriet Zinnes. Reprinted by permission.

"Blue Clothes" and "By the Sea" by Kim Chi Ha are from *The Middle Hour.* Trans. by David R. McCann (Earl M. Coleman Enterprises, Inc., Stanfordville, N.Y.). Copyright by the publisher. Reprinted by permission.

"A Pastoral" by John Ashbery is from *Some Trees,* copyright 1956 by John Ashbery. All rights reserved. Reprinted by permission of the author and George Borchard, Inc.

Photo by Gerard Melanga

Expository and Aesthetic Writing

Ignorance of the difference between expository and aesthetic writing may contribute to a faulty poem. The best prose approaches poetry because it embodies its techniques -- structural patterns, special rhythms, and imagery -- but generally speaking expository prose is writing which does not consider special structural patterns, heightened rhythms, multiple meanings, sound structures, or beats. Its intention generally is to present information. It is known as <u>non-fiction</u>, and it is supposed to deal in facts. Some examples of expository writing are: science texts, journalistic writing, and law treatises.

Aesthetic writing is writing as an art. It is characterized by emotion and by imagery. The best aesthetic writing becomes literature. It is known as fiction, and it is concerned with the imagination. Some examples of aesthetic writing are: poetry, short stories, novels, plays.

It must be borne in mind that aesthetic writing also deals with truth, but it presents a reality different from the reality of physical facts.

When setting out on a study of creative writing, it is helpful to choose a <u>theme</u>. This must not be adhered to as an absolute, but <u>it</u> can be evocative and encompassing and create a central unifying idea. In time, an organic collection of work will exist. Choose your own theme if you wish. For this basic study and for the purpose of clarity, our theme will be Tides.

Our first exercise will help us to recognize and remember the difference between <u>expository</u> and <u>aesthetic</u> writing.

Exercise

EXPOSITORY WRITING

Make a list of facts concerning the tides. Use the dictionary, encyclopedia, or other reference works to obtain your information. In expository prose, write a brief essay called "TIDES."

Example of Expository Writing on Topic, "Tides"

Tides are caused by the gravitational pull of the moon or sun. As the earth spins, it tosses water, which the moon or sun attracts. During the new or full moon, the tides are high. The Spring tides generally are high tides. The sun, moon and earth are, as it were, lined up. High tides exist on both sides of the earth. The tides circulate as the moon revolves. When the moon and sun stand at right angles to the water, we have neap tide. The ebb tide, sometimes called low tide, occurs before the time of change.

AESTHETIC WRITING

Ask yourself how the word, tides, may be used imaginatively to denote other regions of experience besides the rise and fall of the waters. For example, there are tides in emotion, in the realm of life and death, in each day's experience, in love, and in the seasons.

Make notes concerning such a situation which began, had its high point, and dissolved.

Using those notes, write a paragraph of poetic prose or a free poem concerned with that experience. Remember to use images and emotion.

Since this is the first poem of the series, it must not be judged stringently as to special techniques. Later you may wish to revise it.

Example of Aesthetic Writing: "Tides"

Suave surfers are gliding on the sea, but I have my back to the water, and I cannot see the green-bird kite trembling against azure skies. It flies, secured by a single string. If I snip it, it will not sink." Shhh... l l l," whispered the sea. "Close the eyes. See me with ears... Hear what I have to tell...Stay..." said the sea, "taste me, not with tongues, but with the whole of being. Fall into my arms..." "Breathe...," said the sea. "I was your mother."

Bright light radiated. Oceans roared...

Elements of the Poet's Concern

1. The Word

It is the word which raises the human being above the realm of the mineral, the plant, the animal. Man is distinguished from those realms by his capacity to use the word in its multiple nuances as a creative force. <u>Hamlet</u> could be created from combinations of the twenty-six letters in the alphabet. Since essence and dignity are integral to the word, the poet must in no way join those who would debase it. On the contrary, it is he who must enhance the language of his time.

2. Sound

The poet must become concerned with the affective quality of sound, recognizing how different sound combinations evoke certain soul states. As the painter becomes adept in the use of his tools -- paints, leads, textures of paper, brushes, etc. -- the poet must learn how to combine sound and sound, syllable and syllable, word and word, sentence and sentence, in order to express his vision and experience in the most ingenious way.

3. Imagery

It is as natural for images to arise within the human being as for a plant to give forth flowers. Imagery, the very essence of poetry, helps transform the naturalistic experience into art, thus making it valid for all. Each is an individual who may learn to draw aside those opaque shrouds of death -- slogans, cliches, and all the other manipulative abstractions of the media -- and imbue language once again with living force and truth. Images are signs -- bridges to another reality.

4. Tone

Tone is the emotional texture of the poem -- the atmosphere, mood, feeling quality. In oral speech or reading, tone may be indicated by the pitch, modulation, or volume of the voice. To avoid incorrect interpretations, the poet must have knowledge of those elements which will project the intended tone, because the poem is an evocative vessel of multiple meaning in a contracted form, and therefore, misunderstandings may easily result.

5. Rhythm

Rhythm which is connected with the breathing organism, the circulation of the blood, the feeling realm, contains that magic element which can raise the everyday experience to the mantric level. Rhythm in human beings is related to the revolution of the planets and constellations, day transforming to night, the seasonal cycles, the rise and fall of sun and moon, the sweep of oceans and rivers. The poet learns to listen to the inner music of all experience, so that he may transform this into art. Each poet has an individual rhythm, and it is through the manifestation of this rhythm in his work that one recognizes what is known as style. Unintended dissonance is eliminated when the outer and inner ear become tuned.

6. Metre

Metre and rhythm are two different aspects of poetry. Rhythm is an inner flow related to the breathstream and blood circulation; metre is related to the beating of the heart. The Greek poets were masters of metre who knew how to evoke terror and compassion in their audiences by nuances of metre, and they left us a heritage of over thirty metrical possibilities. The poet should learn from the past as a foundation on which to build the present and the future. In our time, there are no set rules for metrical patterns, and the poet may even create his own in consonance with his skill and ingenuity.

7. Rhyme

Rhyme is part of the sound structure of the poem. It is the matching of similar sounds in order to create <u>a verbal texture</u>. At present, rhyme is not an essential of verse making, but it may be used to enhance a desired effect. Ancient scribes knew how rhyme, as a kind of magic, could awaken emotion arising from the unconscious. Rhyme is many-faceted and may be used to evoke multiple meanings.

8. Appeal to the Senses

The written poem on the page is a corpse until it is encountered by a reader. Then the words which, until that moment, seem nothing but little black squiggles, assume the magic potency to change the breath, heartbeat, and sometimes the will and the thoughts of the reader. In order that this may take place, the writer must know how to evoke sense experience artistically so that complex states of being may be expressed poignantly.

9. Structure

Formlessness is anarchy, chaos, a form of **death**. As a work of ceramics is not merely the amorphous clay dredged up from the river, but an embodied organic being created with the thoughts, inspiration, warmth and will of the ceramist, so a poem must be structured into an organic whole. Learning elements of structure makes possible the bringing forth of harmonious beings, not destructive distortions. Dissonance must be intentional to create desired effects, not due to ignorance. In our time the possibilities of structural patterns are infinite. The poem itself will determine its own structure if the poet becomes tuned to its nuances.

10. Spacing

Spacing is an element of structure. The placement of the poem on the page must not be arbitrary, but so conceived that it contributes to the emotional impact. To learn what weaves in silences and pauses is to create a vehicle for the immaterial to enter into and enrich the conscious experience.

11. Punctuation

Punctuation is an element of tone. Rules of punctuation are fairly recent in the development of language. The poet is not required to abide by strict standards of punctuation, necessary for prose communication. The poem is a creation, and punctuation is part of the material which the poet has at his disposal in the formation of that creation. However, to omit punctuation arbitrarily is inexcusable. There must be a good reason for every inclusion or omission.

12. Intention

Poems may describe or teach, express an emotion or an idea, or they may tell a story. It is important to examine the raw material of the poem to determine what it intends, in order to avoid confusion, and in order that one may determine which techniques will best express that intention.

The foregoing elements will be pursued in detail in the following pages. Work carefully with the information, and the exercises will yield gratifying results.

Intention

Many people who write poetry neglect to ask: What is the intention of this particular poem?

This may give rise to contradictions and confusion. To decide on a particular intention and then write a poem to fit it would be deadly. This is the propaganda school of poetry or the poetry of birthday parties. Usually, some inspiring experience will give rise to the poem, but it does not emerge whole and complete. When the first inspiration is recorded and the structuring and expansion begin, the poet should examine his work and try to determine what it intends. Then, with certain knowledge, he can begin to mold it so that it expresses that intention in the most artistic way possible.

What is meant by the Intention?

A poem may express various experiences:

1. It may describe a scene, a person, an experience.

2. It may express an emotion.

3. It may present an idea.

4. It may move to action.

5. It may enlarge a vision of life.

6. It may tell a story.

7. It may teach a lesson.

8. It may sing a song.

9. It may be a mantram.

Examples of Intention

POEM DESCRIBING A SCENE

The Barn on Seven Stars Road

This is the ramshackles ark
Where the rapscallion crow
Cracks his ribald jokes
And the lone dove
    Murmurs vespers

            under mulberry eaves.

    Sun roosts in the rafters;
    Shade broods in the beams;
    And the raggle-taggle winds
    Weave a wistful harmony
    Upon the reeds of shingle.
This is the building built
To shelter and store;
This is the cathedral
Of alfalfa and lamb.

            To enter here
            You would stoop
            Beneath forsythia's blaze
            And snapdragon's brand
            And grow your eyes   accustomed
                                         to dance.

            To wait here
            You would hold your peace
            As dearly as the empty bin
            Holds a hermit mustard seed.

You too would be a barn.
A construction of beams...
And light
Would wake like the rifflings of wings
    In the stillness of the stall.

POEM EXPRESSING AN EMOTION

The Little Mermaid

Will the little blue light be lit by immersion in water
Now that I am dashed back into a midnight ocean
Trying to keep afloat, as they say?

How many trials we endured, who had fallen to whining
And the worship of idols like the Daughters of Moab;
My tail transmuted to legs, my voice
Usurped; the icy winds, the thousand foot waves; and I
with my liver gnawed by mice, danced on daggers on the path
Of white lines, for your iron eyes
Among the peasants who had come for a Sunday outing
To stare at my green face: One two three step! One two three turn!
There was something not understood by me or them.

I scrutinized the wedding guests one by one. The vultures
Were wheeling. I turned, waved, mounted the steps, entered the
    barque.
Now, the inside of the sky extends
Blazing centrifugal rays. Ah, there are the Daughters
Of the Air, closer than friends, closer even than breathing.
They see my tears. My thoughts become feathers.

POEM WHICH ENLARGES A VISION OF LIFE

The Pleiades

Through the crude ceiling
(boughs of blue spruce)
winter stars sparkle on the tines, seven sisters
seven sisters hiding from Orion,
making the night poignant.

That is our comfort:
even the recognition
of evil confirms us.

Daytimes, when the queen star
blinds our bones with love,
the constellations change.
Nights, wanting the world ruly,
we say no laws are altered.

Yet, how sweet it is
to pinpoint the Pleiades
when you are alone.

POEM WHICH TELLS A STORY

Ambiguous connection:

The Complete Story

1.
Barriers in these streets;
barred the doors.
The empty envelope
without return address
has been dispatched
to the Office of Dead Letters.

Yet in the pauses rise
the images of stopped motion
called:
    The Embrace
    The Offense
    The Dismissal
    The Avalanche:
seals for eternity
whose lineaments
time and absence
do not erase
but rather incise.

2.
Cracked the instrument:
the strings coil
like thin worms.
If you listen you will hear
the wind in the hollow
make a frail moan.

  It doesn't matter
  in any case
  now that the hands are severed.

3.
Let us go back to the beginning:
    The door opens:
      the eloquent hands which take one in:
      the illumined tree:
      piano music from an open window.

The ground falls away:
the rope tightens.

4.
When I arrived
you were in the kitchen:
Mouth to beak, you were feeding
a wounded crow in a cage.
Cats were circling the house.

I cried:
    "There is a black crow in a cage in you.
    There is a crow in a cage between us.
    There is a crow with a broken wing in me.
    Let the wounded crow in us be lifted up!"

The next week you came to tell me
you found the crow
you had freed, in the garden,
dead,
- neck cracked by a cat.

5.
Does it matter to the door
if it opens or closes?
Or to the empty chair that faces the linden?
Silence snakes in greyly, opens scars.
It is better to cut the telephone cord.

    The train tracks
    speed more swiftly back to the point of departure,
    the greater the speed of the train
    away from it.

6.
- "The unsent letters arrive," - she said.
- "And what of the unfinished stories?"

    - "They will be taken up again.
    Though we walk off in opposite directions.
    we walk in a circle
    back to the point of encounter
    where every story is resumed."

POEM WHICH TEACHES A LESSON

Flight

1.
Birds' wings are spread:
birds do not spread wings.

Birds do not choose to fly:
birds are placed in flight.

We can choose to ignite
or to ignore what might
kindle us to flight.

2.
Will mountains flow?
Will rooted trees dance?
Could we with bones of marrow
advance to fly?

We'll fly
When we wake
To the why
Of walk.

POEM AS SONG

Song

Leave: say never

    Leave: say never:
and I will gather
myrtle and rue:
    adorn my bed
with branches of trailing yew.

    Think me away:
say sapphire ever,
and I will cower:
    cover my head:
wither the heart's flower:

    and the rose fade too:
double my woe:
and I will weave
    gray cloud veils
to shroud the sky into winter.

>   Sever: and I will intone
> wails so minor,
> lark will fall
>   and snow cover all
> except nettle and willow.
>
> O, a shroud and a thorn-crown, ash and bone
> for my love has gone, saying: never, ever.

POEM AS MANTRAM

> The seeds sprout in the womb of Earth,
> The rains stream from heights of heaven;
> So love sprouts in human hearts,
> and wisdom streams into human thoughts.

Exercise

1. Determine the intentions of any poems you have written.

2. Outline a series of exercises in which you attempt to fulfill some of the above intentions. Keep the poem unified. (Remember these are merely exercises.)

3. Using an anthology or volume of poetry, try to determine the intentions of individual poems therein.

Stream of Consciousness

How may the poet develop into a poem, a line in his journal, a feeling expressed poetically but not completed, an observation, an idea, particularly when time has passed since the original recording of the experience? This is a major problem for the developing writer.

In the early part of the century, the Surrealists developed what they called the <u>Stream of Consciousness</u> or <u>Automatic Writing</u>. They sought to tap that source from which imagery springs, and they knew this was not from the abstract intellect. From their study of dreams, they noted that dream imagery had similar symbolic significance as poetic imagery, and they attempted to bring that imagery into the waking state. A line, a word, an idea, was placed in the center of one's attention. Then whatever suggested itself was written down without thought to logical sequence, punctuation, sentence structure or organized form. It was discovered that poetic imagery flows forth from the unconscious with a logic of its own.

Such a procedure is a good way to arrive at the level of poetic experience which is not the naturalistic. But there is a danger. Many young poets began to believe that whatever emerged was considered as the finished poem. This would be equivalent to dredging clay from the river and considering the lump on the shore to be a great work of sculpture. In this way, many distortions entered the realm of the arts. The material of the stream is the raw material which the artist must mold into form through his skill, love, and thought. If one bears that in mind, the technique may be useful.

Exercise

Take a word which has to do with the theme "Tides" and write a free stream of consciousness, allowing the images to flow without hindrance from the pen. You will note that memory plays a leading role here. Do not consciously consider sentence structure or logical sequence.

When you have done this, <u>study</u> the result. Do you detect a main <u>idea</u> or major <u>image</u> in the notes?

<u>Underline</u> those images which are pertinent to the major theme.

<u>Eliminate</u> what has no bearing.

Now try to <u>organize</u> the experience into a finished poem. You may have to do some rearranging of lines.

Rewrite as many times as necessary, being attentive to the form which seeks to be embodied in the final work.

Meditated Stream of Consciousness

A more advanced method, and one perhaps more in keeping with modern consciousness is the meditated stream of consciousness. Here thinking is used in such a way that it becomes living, imaginative, inspired. This procedure consists of the following method:

Place a word, an idea, or an experience like a seed in the center of your consciousness.

Now meditate on it with awareness, rather than as a chance experience. Don't attempt to allow the onrush of interfering and irrelevant thoughts to disturb the stream of your concentration. Allow that central seed to begin to tell its own story, but in a focussed way.

Exercise

Take the word "seed," or "sand," or "foam," and attempt the above technique.

Once the initial work is recorded, follow the same procedure as previously. Don't be discouraged if in the beginning the poetic images take time to emerge. Be persistent and surely, finally, they will appear.

EXAMPLE OF A MEDITATED STREAM OF
CONSCIOUSNESS ON TIDES

Tides... rhythmic movements of water... All of life has tides... It is the breathing of the waters... the heaving of the sea... Is the earth, the sea alive? Are they living beings? The moon is connected with the tides... everyone knows that. Surely all the stars and planets are also involved... At neap tide, we are able to stand at right angles to the water. I never had heard of neap tide before now. It's a beautiful thought. Ebb tide... I see the sand and there are designs like tree forms and continents which the waves later erase. These designs seem to have harmonious shapes, most beautiful... There are shapes of birds, and maps... of which places

Some Uses of Imagery

1. To achieve vividness and concreteness in expressing feeling, conviction; an experience, not a general statement, is conveyed.

2. To unify the fractured and separated, to unite seemingly unexpected relationships, to achieve a new unity and thereby an expansion of consciousness.

3. To enforce unity by means of parallels; two comparable situations are set up, one serving as the metaphoric equivalent of the other.

4. To convey ideas in an unabstract manner.

5. To convey subtle states of feeling through shadings made possible by imagery.

6. To embody tensions of opposites: contrasts, movement, change.

7. To create rhythms by repetition of key images: harmonies, reverberations of meaning.

8. To reveal new aspects of objects, people, situations.

The Image and the Symbol

Much has been written concerning the difference between the image and the symbol. Some major differences will be indicated:

An image is a comparison which may be used once or even a few times, and which relates to a particular experience without necessarily having a profound significance.

The symbol occurs when, in a body of work, an image is repeated and emphasized to imply that it stands for a profound experience in the life and work of the author.

Imagery may be directly descriptive or metaphoric, joining unlike things at their point of resemblance.

A symbol may be a free metaphor whose meaning is not necessarily limited. A symbol may contain several images.

Objective and Subjective Imagery

<u>Objective Imagery</u>: Precise notations of objective reality. 'The soul' is omitted. The Imagists attempted to use this technique.

<u>Example</u>: The leaves fall.

No comparison, no complex experience rising from the unconscious is expressed.

<u>Subjective Imagery</u>: Elements of objective reality are combined with images rising from the unconscious, often with loose mysterious connections as in dreams, in order to evoke inner turmoil and feeling. The Surrealists carried this to extremes by recording untransformed irrational dream imagery.

<u>Example</u>: "Am I a house accursed, cursing and feeding on dead rosemary?"

A poem may be <u>hermetic</u>, revealing itself after much contemplation. However, <u>obscurity</u> -- that is, being utterly private and personal so that it can never have meaning for a reader other than the author himself -- is unacceptable.

In using subjective imagery, there exists a danger that the poem may become indecipherable. However, the subjective experience in the hands of a true artist becomes universal.

A POEM USING OBJECTIVE IMAGERY

Fear

Two eyes heave out
A man groans.
Two birds fly
A feather falls.
One boy rolls one stone.

Some Characteristics of Imagery and Symbol

<u>Cultural image</u>: relates to a common experience in a particular culture. If the reader has been brought up in a different cultural background, he will have to do research in order to understand the image. Example: "I felt like Hester Prynne in the *Scarlet Letter*."

<u>Universal image</u>: images which people anywhere and everywhere would understand. Example: imagery associated with the stars, the sun, and the moon.

<u>Archetypal image or symbol</u>: images found in all societies in all epochs, and associated with myths, religions, rituals. These images arise out of the human unconscious, often called the "collective unconscious;" they reveal basic human patterns of behavior and experience. Example: The <u>Hero</u> sets forth on a <u>journey</u> to find the <u>Golden Fleece</u>. (The hero is the individual whose life is a journey to find the higher self or the transformation of consciousness.)

<u>Classical imagery</u>: images from ancient or classical times, or from the neo-classical period in the early eighteenth century.

<u>Example</u>: Softly sweet, in Lydian measures
Soon he soothed his soul to pleasures.

John Dryden, *Alexander's Feast*

<u>Romantic imagery</u>: imagery from the so-called Romantic period in the late eighteenth and early nineteenth centuries.

<u>Example</u>: O wild west wind, thou breath of autumn's being
Thou, from whose unseen presence the leaves dead
Are driven, like ghosts from an enchanter fleeing...

Percy B. Shelley, *Ode to the West Wind*

<u>Contemporary imagery</u>: metaphors which could not have appeared in literature of the past, but which relate to contemporary experience. In the neo-classical period rules were established which circumscribed what was and what was not accepted as poetry, but the dissonances of modern life and consciousness are now accepted. Surrealism, Dada, and other literary movements, at their best, tended to liberate the possibilities of expression.

Example: Let us go then you and I
           When the evening is spread out against the sky
           Like a patient etherized upon a table...

> T. S. Eliot, *The Love Song of
> J. Alfred Prufrock*

<u>An Anachronism</u>: an image which could not have existed in the time of the setting of the poem; for example, the inclusion of a television set in a poem about Ancient Greece which was not meant to create a special effect.

<u>A Mixed Metaphor</u>: when the poet unintentionally destroys the unity of the poem by including unrelated metaphors. For special dissonant effects, this may be useful, but not because of ignorance.

<u>A Pathetic Fallacy</u>: when oversentimentality is employed in personifying.

Example: "The darling faces of the little pansies
           stared at me and smiled."

EXAMPLE OF CONTEMPORARY IDIOM

Living Space

When the body is flattened
and folded back with the bed
at the advent of clock change
and vanishes into the couch
you can bet your moon it's time.
Yes. But there's no need to cry
"I'm crushed," even though
the coils press
just sing out like a good ghost
and when the cushions
muffle your voice
Sing louder.

POEMS USING ARCHETYPAL IMAGERY

Instructions for Search

point your hands like a compass to down
and dive off the edge of madagascar
into the tea-warm indian ocean

as the fathoms widen before you
in a blue-green peacock's tail
elongate yourself like an eel
round and flat at the same time
then move your arms in great arcs
and descend along the path of broken sunlight

swim carefully through the hypnotizing seaweed
over the ragged battlements of tulip-colored corals
until at last, you pass
the ironwork of the continent
and you are below the world.

here where the sun is repulsed by the fist of pressure
blind fish like beggars wait for alms
and the sea is a buddha silent and dark

    no progression
    no regression
    fullness flatness of tides
    the eye in the throat beats the time
    when the pupil is ready
    the teacher arrives

        wait
    for the coelacanth
    fish of rounded gills and lobed fins
    400 million years old
    last inhabitant of the devonian sea

    if he approaches
        unseen
        unheard

    ask him

    how did you survive?

Seduction

The swirl of the cosmic cape
scarlet
distracts the eye
shields the sword.

Five yards apart,
the distance between stars.
The lure of Venus
The fire of Taurus.

The promise forgotten.
Six arrows pierce the neck
of the war god.
Tipped with sunlight
spotted with blood,
a peacock's fan.
From the lonely call of the trumpet,
silence,
the alliance.

Death glides
to the right, to the left, to the right
A lunge, a parry
Tempts, teases,
bends close, closer
circles on itself.

Molten rage swells Taurus
Venus postures rigid, detached.
Thrust, reposte
blood passes one to the other.
They wind
scraping the dry dust
tightening the circle of their lives.

A thrust
completes the triad
and makes one God
the other dust.

POEM USING CLASSICAL IMAGERY

In The Rif Mountains
(Northern Morocco)

Geology set this story down so long ago
it's a wonder it's still legible.
But the stylized hand is still clearly Arabic,
dark against the pale tan tablets of mountainside.

The violence of what's being told is belied
by the formal language of old rock,
as is the case with the later chronicles
written by, and about, smaller convulsions, men.
How shapely the various grammars that record
the brief cycles in which our substance roils and cools.
And the violence in each case is belied
a second time: the elegant calligraphy of rock and quill.

Yet close-to, the running, friable stone,
leached and pitted, no longer looks like writing
but like the spotted backs of old geology's hands.
They rest, translucent, calm, the dreadful story told
and left here on these slanting tablets
for the tribes that will presently enter.

The tribes enter. They read the rocks as their Homer--
the source of a thousand years of manners,
the model for the heats and seisms
that will harden into the Rifs of their dynasties
and then erode to build the foothills of their blood,
as it has been told.

Figures of Speech

Some images are called figures of speech. In this basic course four types will be discussed: The Simile, the Metaphor, the Personification, the Hyperbole.

1. <u>The Simile</u>: A comparison using the words "like" or "as."

   <u>Example</u>: What a piece of work is man!...
   In action how like an angel! In apprehension
   How like a God!

   - William Shakespeare; *Hamlet*

2. <u>The Metaphor</u>: a comparison of two unlike things without the use of "like" or "as." The metaphor tends to be more evocative and dynamic. In everyday life metaphors are often used which have become cliches:

   "He is a pig."

   "She's a chicken."

   "You're a pest."

   <u>Example</u>: This precious stone set in a silver sea (about England)

   - William Shakespeare; *Richard II*

3. <u>The Personification</u>: a special type of metaphor which gives human traits to inanimate objects. In colloquial usage people say:

   "the arms of a chair"

   "the hands of a clock"

   "the legs of a table"

   <u>Example</u>: Methought the billows spoke and told me of it;
   The winds did sing it to me; and the thunder
   That deep and dreadful organ-pipe, pronounced
   The name of Prospero...

   - William Shakespeare; *The Tempest*

POEM USING PERSONIFICATION

The Ballad of the Water of the Sea

The sea
smiles from far away.
Teeth of foam,
lips of sky.

- What do you sell, oh, dusky maid,
with your breasts in the wind?

- I sell, senor, the water
of the seas.

What do you bear, oh black young man,
mingled with your blood?

I bear, senor, the water
of the seas.

- These salty tears,
from where do they come, mother?

- I weep, senor, the water
of the seas.

- Heart; and this bitterness
so deep, where was it born?

- Bitter indeed, the water
of the seas.

The sea
smiles from far away.
Teeth of foam,
lips of sky.

4. <u>The Hyperbole</u>: an exaggeration to achieve a particular effect. American humor is based on hyperbole: There is the famous fish story; or Johnny Appleseed who went across the states scattering appleseeds; and many more. Slapstick and the humor of clowns are based on hyperbole. In colloquial speech we have:

>"I was starving to death."
>
>"You're killing me!"
>
>"We laughed so hard we were splitting our sides."

<u>Example</u>:

>Blow winds, and crack your cheeks! Rage! Blow!
>You cataracts and hurricanes, spout
>Till you have drenched our steeples, drowned
> the cocks!
>You sulphurous and thought-executing fires,
>Vaunt couriers to oak-cleaving thunderbolts,
>Singe my white head! And thou, all-shaking
> thunder,
>Strike flat the thick rotundity of the world!
>Crack nature's mounds, all germins spill at once
>That make ungrateful man!"
>
>   William Shakespeare, *King Lear*

POEM USING SIMILE

>from, the sea
>
>
>bull seals
>
>fight on the sea
>
>like vicious old ladies
>
>at tea furious
>
>over trivialities

POEM USING HYPERBOLE AND DELICATE EMOTION

Translations From the Russian

Dearest
how frail, how fragile you are
giant woman, Mother
larger than mytho-
logical years
in a world of epidemics
out of control like
my whooping cough hacking across
New York ferry, passing summers
back and forth to the Statue of Liberty
always saying goodbye to me
as though I were
safe

Dearest
how frail, how fragile you are
entering my house now
with a noise so different
that pictures rattle
on my wall. Even Picasso's Blue Period
fades. O Mother
who tried learning English
in classes for foreigners, U.S.A.
but finding easy
all needful rites, food, love
rituals that stay
honorable like parts of history
bringing your face
lined with Pushkin, Gorki, Tolstoy
ten times seven dreams away
where private wounds began reporting
battles of whatever happens
must happen, pushing through
some heroic contest, x-ray shadows
plain near the heart's artery
stopping for breath

> I kiss you
> as you keep melting
> into a background of terrible
> flowers that choke me
> where you walk, thick shoe
> stepping, swaying like
> a sisal rope losing strength
> but certain
> in ways a great river has to go
> full flood
> forward, forward

Exercises

1. Simile

    a. Make a list of colloquial similes.

    b. Using the theme Tides, write five similes:

    The ocean was like.....
    The ship was like .....
    The beach was like.....
    The storm was like.....
    The moon on the waves was like.....

    When writing figures of speech, be very specific: Think of a particular ship, a particular place, a particular time. Do not generalize.

    c. Rearrange and organize the above into a poem. Give it a title. (Remember, this is an exercise in developing imagination and form.)

2. Metaphor

    a. Change the above similes into metaphors by omitting the word 'like.'

    b. Rearrange and organize these into a poem. (Do not hesitate to add new examples.)

3. Personification

    a. Make a list of colloquial personifications.

    b. Rearrange and organize into a poem.

4. Hyperbole

    a. Make a list of colloquial hyperboles.

    b. Write five hyperboles associated with the topic "Tides."

    c. Rearrange and organize into a poem.

POEM WITH VARIOUS FIGURES OF SPEECH

On the Seashore

On the seashore of endless worlds children meet.
  The infinite sky is motionless overhead
and the restless water is boisterous. On the
seashore of endless worlds the children meet
with shouts and dances.

They built their houses with sand, and
they play with empty shells. With withered
leaves they weave their boats and smilingly
float them on the vast deep. Children have
their play on the seashore of worlds.

They know not how to swim, they know
not how to cast nets. Pearl-fishers dive for
pearls, merchants sail in their ships, while
children gather pebbles and scatter them
again. They seek not for hidden treasures,
they know not how to cast nets.

The sea surges up with laughter, and pale
gleams the smile of the sea-beach. Death-
dealing waves sing meaningless ballads to the
children, even like a mother while rocking
her baby's cradle. The sea plays with children, and pale gleams the smile of the sea-
beach.

On the seashore of endless worlds children
meet. Tempest roams in the pathless sky,
ships are wrecked in the trackless water,
death is abroad and children play. On the
seashore of endless worlds is the great meeting
of children.

Looking back at the above figures of speech, create a well organized poem including several of each, or create new ones. Take time to combine, select, rearrange, omit. Give the poem a title. You will note that you will have a rather unusually good poem, even though it has been contrived.

5. When the poem is completed, ask yourself the following questions:

   a. Did I avoid the cliche?

   b. Are my images original, drawn from my concentration and contemplation?

   c. Is the poem unified? If so, what is the unifier?

   d. Is my title original? (Titles in poetry are important since they often hold the clue to the poem's meaning, and they may also serve as unifying factor.)

6. Study poems in books and try to identify the figures of speech. Write the figures of speech you discover with their identifying title.

Imagery of Waking Consciousness, Memory, and Dream

Waking consciousness, memory, and dream are three different states of human experience. The possibilities of expressing experience will be greatly enhanced if the poet learns to be attentive to the kind of imagery evoked by those states.

WAKING CONSCIOUSNESS

Events seem logical, linear.
Objects have names which are recognized in similar ways
  by normal people.
Color, line, texture, location, shape may be described
  objectively.
The five senses play a major role.
The ego directs action.

MEMORY

Memory filters, selects.
One may sense that the memory is connected with the heart and lung region, not with the head.
Gravity is lifted.
There is an absence of sense detail.
Essence remains and is subjectively experienced impressionistically. This tends to be so even when experience which originally caused pain is remembered.
Time sequence is not sequential, yet distortions as in dreams are not prevalent.
More feeling than thought is involved.
Fantasy and wishful thinking or day dreaming tend to become mixed with reality.

DREAMS

The impossible becomes possible.
A kind of vertical sight sets in; for example, one may see as from above -- trees, lake, houses. Three dimensional perspective does not exist.
Time is psychological rather than chronological. Persons of the past mingle with those of the present.
Space also interweaves in metamorphosing ways.
Places mingle, cross, blend.
Gravity of waking consciousness is not existant.
There is distortion, surprise, illogicality, incongruity, extremes.
In dreams the ego leaves the body and does not participate as a regulator or determinant of the experience.
To record dreams is an excellent training for the writer.

A POEM OF WAKING OBSERVATION

    Contemplations: the lake

    Sun in water
    shatters in the current
    feathering wings.

    rainbow clouds on water
    quiver: spiral out.
    illusory depth.

    (the diamond:
    prism: white sun
    in shimmering rainbow.)

water breaks
and rearranges
design of substance.

first withered leaves
(some die young)
float slowly.

a falcon planes,
pauses:
tremor of wings.

a jubilant lark
hovers high:
dives earthward.

a dragonfly
- wings of light -
skims over the lake.

birds call: busy birdcalls:
different
from songs of evening.

POEM USING IMAGERY OF MEMORY

The Ghosts of Jersey City

Down the long farways, shabby streets of shingled houses,
grit alleys, over the backyards and the weedy meadows,
they halloo my longago name.

I do not waken to their call but sleep nostalgic, dream again
the stolid Polish girls in clusters on the high, narrow stoops
clovering the summer night with promise.

I dream that Tully's broken wagons suddenly limp from the
corner lot and roll horseless, lumbering down the cobblestone street
in a last parade, shafts dragging.

Ghosts. Fists and heroes. Boyle's Thirty Acres, and the endless
talk of fights and fighters on street corners, in the barber shops
over the *Police Gazette*.

Sidewalks, and children skipping rope in the street, ramshackle air,
All in together, girls, how do you like the weather, girls,
Doubledutch and hopscotch.

Factory smoke and laughter. Fierce races around the block.
Ringaleevio into the night. Through the redolence of decay,
the warm persistent reek of life.

A POEM IN MEMORY

In the winter city

We take refuge in a duration of late summer:
the isle of Skopolos, that "wunderbarer Traum"
rays into the mists its iridescent dust.
Warm wind wafts the white sails; the bow cleaves the wave
in a vector of turquoise and foam: now ringing
the bare trees in a circle rainbow; singing
counter melodies to traffic and sirens.

Are the Archangels who, over Delphi,
blessed our simultaneous sight with the sign
of the cross crowned in silver, trailing
those veils among the glass coffins of this night
to heighten the double essence of your absence?

The event was that finally, you allowed
history to be created between us:
In silver and shadow near the Castalian Spring
in whose waters the stars were swinging; in green-gold
among the wild goats, under the fig trees and grape arbours,
in Byzantine interiors, - ikon-illumined:
On ships, on beaches, in Cyclopean caves,
our separate images conjoined in the same frame.

Around the city, rise temple columns of light
haloing the noble ancient faces we saw engraved
on the taupe hills, swirling in waters, sailing
the skies. And sometimes as I move through the day,
my lips assume the smile of the Lion of Kea,
my visage, his vision: I walk like caryatids:
my eyes of Charioteer pierce evolving futures,
and I become the essence of space molded by marble.

For that brief enduring sequence, we grew fruitful
like Earth gathering sun for winter to fertilize
her seeds: and like those friezes on steles
of ancient departed, conquering negation,
we gently laid hand upon hand in eternity.

A POEM USING DREAM IMAGERY

Seven Dreams Appear

1.
7 x 7 drunken triangles
Cavort like slick puppets

2.
From Japan to Tibet - moons cast dead rays
This means: Beware of falsity.

3.
Drowning the lark points its toes
Sparrows tweaked in cold and dead trees
The stones stared

4.
Then a loud and fraiding bang
And my feetsteps sound so fear away

5.
In the ring lay the open horses

6.
The curtain had fallen on an act of murder
The miraculous murder of the bouncing ball
And now the stage was set for the last act

7.
May I look into the box of hands to see if I can
   find my hand?

A POEM USING IMAGERY OF DREAM

Curtain Curtain

The roving theatres of the seasons will have played out my life
To my hisses
The Apron had been set as a dungeon from where I could hiss
My hands on the iron bars I watched against a backdrop of black
   foliage
Nude up to her waist the heroine
Who killed herself at the beginning of Act I
Oddly enough the play proceeded in the chandelier
By and by a fog covered the stage
At times I cried out
I smashed the jug they had given me butterflies flew out
And rose crazily toward the chandelier
Pretending to be a ballet interlude performed by my thoughts
I attempted to cut open my wrist with shards of the brown jug
But these were countries where I was lost
I could not find the thread of those voyages
I was cut off by this loaf of sun
A character moved about the theatre the only character in motion
Who wore a mask of my face
To my disgust he was for the villain and for the ingenue
It was rumored that it had been planned like May June July and August
Suddenly the cavern became deeper
In the interminable passages bouquets held shoulder high
Wandered about by themselves I scarcely dared open my door
I had been granted too much freedom all at once
Freedom to escape in the sleigh of my bed
Freedom to revive the persons I miss
The aluminum chairs closed ranks around a kiosk of mirrors
A curtain rose dew-fringed with blood turned green
Freedom to expel the semblance of reality
The stage trap was marvelous on a white wall appeared
  a stippled engraving of fire my silhouette pierced in the heart
  by a bullet

Exercises

1. Take a flower -- a rose, for example. Observe it. Touch it. Smell it. Study the colors of the petals, etc. Note its shape, its gesture. Write a description of this rose. (Use figures of speech.)

2. Place the rose aside and try to recall an experience in which a rose played a major role: a birthday, funeral, party, appointment, etc. Write about this experience as a memory, always focussing on the rose as the unifying factor.

3. Create a dream experience of a rose. Remember in a dream the rose may become grotesque, may assume animal forms, etc.

Note the difference in tone of the above three exercises. Try to create a finished poem from the experience involved.

4. Record a dream. Study its imagery, symbols, emotion, mood. Organize the experience into a poem.

5. Write a contrived dream poem concerning some aspect of the theme, Tides.

When poems are read in the future, you will discover that previously incomprehensible works will become clear when you realize them as awake, memory, or dream experience.

The Appeal to the Senses

A particular kind of imagery is known as the <u>Appeal to the Senses</u>. To appeal to the senses means learning to place sense-engaging sounds, words, and sentences together in such a way that they evoke an experience of objective or subjective reality in which the reader may participate. A kind of magic is involved. It is interesting to consider why in ancient times only highly initiated scribes were permitted to write, and any layman who dared to attempt it was put to death.

Such imagery produces a wide range of sensory effects; these appeal to the five senses with which most people are familiar: hearing, sight, touch, taste, smell. But there are seven other senses to which they appeal. These <u>twelve senses</u> are:

1. The sense of the <u>Ego</u>: Only an individual can say "I," recognizing himself as a separate individual from another.

2. <u>Thought</u> sense: having the ability to form thoughts and the ability to observe one's own thoughts.

3. <u>Word</u> sense: the ability to form words and to grasp their meaning.

4. Sense of <u>hearing</u>: hearing with the ear, but also with the inner ear.

5. Sense of <u>sight</u>.

6. <u>Warmth</u> sense: having the ability to feel warmth, both physically and in the soul realm.

7. <u>Taste</u>.

8. <u>Smell</u>.

9. <u>Touch</u>.

10. Sense of <u>Balance</u>.

11. Sense of <u>Movement</u>.

12. <u>Life</u> sense.

In this basic course, we will concentrate on the five senses with which most people are familiar: hearing, sight, touch, taste, smell.

Hearing

Human beings have a certain range within which sound is audible. Animals, as most people know, have a much larger range of audibility. Some musicians have what is known as, "perfect pitch." They are able to distinguish the tiniest errors in musical interpretations. They are <u>audio directed</u>. To train oneself to develop a wider range of hearing requires great discipline. Blind people are bombarded with noise, but their lack of sight forces them to learn to distinguish sounds. It is a fact that the general level of hearing among young people has been seriously lowered.

There are different ways in which one may appeal to the sense of hearing:

1. One may relate an experience mainly through the <u>sounds</u> connected with it. In the short story, <u>"The Birthday Party</u>," a sick child in an adjoining room hears the sounds of the party, and experiences it more intensely than those present.

2. Emotional states affect our senses in different ways. By focusing on the effects of emotional experiences on the physical body and the feelings, and particularly on the sense of hearing, a powerful description may result. For example, if you recall how your hearing was affected by a situation of terror and describe this, an experience of terror may be evoked in the reader.

3. One must train oneself to become attentive to the tone which issues from living beings: bird cries, a bark, a voice: Are they expressing joy or despair? Then one must listen for the sounds of nature, of machines, of cities, forests, beaches, and learn to distinguish individual sounds from amorphous noise.

There are several theories connected with the origin of language. The most plausible is recorded in Genesis, and this is further expressed in The Gospel of St. John:

"In the beginning was the Word." These beliefs imply a primal origin of language, and state that, if a person is highly attuned, he will give forth the primal word which will define an experience.

Another belief is the <u>Ding Dong Theory</u> which projects the idea that language originated through imitation of sounds heard.

Then there is the <u>Bow Wow Theory</u> which implies that out of the clicks and clacks and other animal sounds, human language evolved.

In the following exercises, when words appealing to the sense of hearing are called for, rather than making a statement like, "I hear footsteps," try to find suitable words which have suitable sounds inherent within them. Such descriptive words are known as *Onomatopoeia*. There are two kinds of Onomatopoeia:

1. <u>Actual words</u> which imitate the sounds expressed, which have become standard.

<u>Examples</u>: murmur, whisper, ringing

2. <u>Made-up words</u> which attempt to imitate the sounds:

<u>Examples</u>: Ding dong, bow wow, plop

Exercises

1. There are words which have inherent within them sounds of the experience described.

There are many sounds around us at every moment. Close your eyes and listen, then record what sounds you hear within the room and without. Find the vivid word to describe it.

2. Try to find words for various sounds you create. Jingle some keys and try to create a sound for this. Stamp around the room, bang a door, then find sounds to describe these. These onomatopoetic words are particularly effective in expressing humor.

3. Taking ten of the words on the above lists, write an organized paragraph on some aspect of our topic: The Sea. The Storm. The Beach in Summer. The Classroom. You may also make a new list of sound words that are associated with the topic you choose.

4. Recall a particular scene from your life experience. Try to recall clearly the place, atmosphere, time and other circumstances. Be specific. Place this memory in your consciousness and allow it to be written forth in that meditated stream we have already attempted. Recall and list the sounds that may have been associated with the experience. When complete, rearrange, eliminate, structure, and form a poem. Remember, this poem must appeal particularly to the sense of hearing, so use at least five hearing words.

5. Imagine you are witnessing a scene from behind a soundproof glass, a scene such as an explosion which ordinarily would be associated with a great noise. You will note that gravity seems to be dissolved, and a kind of slow motion sets in. For example, if one were witnessing a building falling, the stones would seem to be flying up off the ground. Describe such a scene in words.

6. Goethe speaks of the music of the spheres. There are happenings which occur beyond the realm of physical sound, but we seem to experience them with an inner ear. Make a list of such experiences: For example:

What sound does the snow make melting?

The colors screamed.

The Taj Majal was soft music.

The arpeggios of silver moonlight on
   the water.

Try to carry this experience through into a poem. You will find that wonderful emotional effects may be achieved thus.

                           The Mute

        Do you not hear?
              When I make this warbling
                                  of the fingers,
           This twitter of the wrist as of twigs
                                  in autumn palsy...
        Do you not hear?
              I am speaking of wrens.
           And if my hands make this word, thus:
                 Scooping the air
                    and letting it pour off
                                  the palm
                       in a slow swashbuckle
                                  and slop
                                  and burp
                                  and glug...
                    Is it not clear?
              I am speaking of mud.
           And this word that I mould so:
              Deftly,
                 like the whisper
                            of cartwheeling
                                  sparks...
        Why do you not hear?

        POEM APPEALING   TO THE SENSE OF HEARING

                           Donkeys

   They are not silent like work-horses
   Who are happy or indifferent about the plow and the wagon,
   Donkeys don't submit like that
   For they are sensitive
   And cry continually under their burdens;
   Yes, they are animals of sensibility
   Even if they aren't intelligent enough
   To count money or discuss religion.

   Laugh if you will when they hee-haw
   But know that they are crying
   When they make that noise that sounds like something
   Between a squawking water-pump and a fog-horn.

And when I hear them sobbing
I suddenly notice their sweet eyes and ridiculous ears
And their naive bodies that look as though they never grew up
But stayed children, as in fact they are;
And being misunderstood as children are
They are forced to walk up mountains
With men and bundles on their backs.

Somehow I am glad that they do not submit without a protest
But as their masters are of the deafest
The wails are never heard.

I am sure that donkeys know what life should be
But, alas, they do not own their bodies:
And if they had their own way, I am sure
That they would sit in a field of flowers
Kissing each other, and maybe
They would even invite us to join them.

For they never let us forget that they know
(As everyone knows who stays as sweet as children)
That there is a far better way to spend time;
You can be sure of that when they stop in their tracks
And honk and honk and honk.

Sight

The sense of sight is one of the major senses whereby we encounter and absorb the world around us. Most of the senses we have been concerned with are found in the head organization, and through them, the world communicates with us. It is not only that our eyes record an image; our eyes go out to meet what comes toward us from an object. An insensitive person who is not awake to the world around him will never become a good writer. The lesson on Imagery is closely connected with the sense of sight. In addition, there are other considerations.

Exercises

1. Train yourself to note details in your daily activities. When entering a room to meet people, try to be attentive; recall how they were dressed, what particular gestures they made, their expressions, their eyes, mouth, nose, ears, hair. These observations will eventually give rise to intuitions concerning character, life habits, and experiences:

encounters rise within him, and seven volumes of one of the greatest novels of all time proceed from there.

People have a tendency to overuse the word, "smell."

What some people call "smells" are, strictly speaking, "odors." Actually, the word 'smell' is a verb, not a noun. Only beings with noses can smell. We smell an odor.

Try to be specific when describing various odors. Consider the following substitutes:

1. <u>Fragrance</u>: describes a delicate odor: flowers, perfumes, <u>air</u>, etc.

2. <u>Aroma</u>: describes a strong, pungent odor, usually appealing: coffee, tobacco, steak, pine woods, etc.

3. <u>Stench</u>: describes a strong, nauseating odor: garbage, <u>dead fish</u>, corpses, etc.

4. <u>Stink</u>: This is a slang word for stench which has now been absorbed into the language. It is a cliche when used to describe everything one dislikes, but effective to describe a sickening odor.

5. <u>Scene</u>: This may be used for pleasant or unpleasand odors. It is not as strong as a stench, not as soft as a fragrance: certain perfumes, skunks, soap, etc.

One must make oneself attentive to distinctions and learn to be specific.

Exercises

1. Make a list of words appealing to the sense of smell. Example: delicate, fragrant, nauseating, rotten, metallic, etc.

2. Make a list of odors which you find particularly appealing. You will become aware that human beings have very individual tastes in this area. One can learn a great deal about a person by learning which odors appeal to him.

3. Make a list of those odors you find particularly unpleasant.

Taste

The sense of taste is closely related to the sense of smell. The olfactory nerves are close to the nerves connected with taste, and thus there are many overlapping descriptive words. Actually, taste is more than simply connected with foods, etc. We say a person has taste when he evidences certain judgment in a particular area which is superior.

Inner taste has to do with sharp pungent desires and is closely bound to us.

It is evident that people who work in advertising must have a keen grasp of how one may appeal to these and the other senses, for the word may stir to action, and they know it.

Exercises

1. Make a list of words appealing to the sense of taste. Note how often they also appeal to the sense of smell: bitter, sweet, salty, bland, peppery, hot, piquant, spicey, etc.

2. Try to write a poem called "Picnic," or "My Favorite Meal," or choose another title, and appeal particularly to the senses of taste and smell.

The senses of taste and smell are closely associated with sympathy and antipathy.

Touch

The whole body, not just the fingertips, is an organ of touch. You have only to observe a baby and this will become clear.

Exercises

1. Take a seashell. Close your eyes and feel it. Now try to describe the experience with words. Use a figure of speech, if you wish. Other objects may be

used: a rock, a flower petal, sand, fur, hair.

    2. Make a list of words which appeal to the sense of touch: smooth, rough, sharp, pointed, lumpy, etc.

    3. There was an airplane accident during which the plane landed in mudflats and the passengers wallowed in deep mud and had to drag themselves out. Try to describe such an experience with words.

    4. Write a poem called, "Clay": "A Crown of Thorns," or another that particularly appeals to this sense.

    Excerpt from *The Great Lover* by Ruppert Brooke

These I have loved;
        White plates and cups, clean gleaming.
Ringed with blue lines; and feathery faery dust;
Wet roofs, beneath the lamp-light; the strong crust
Of friendly bread; and many-tasting food;
Rainbows; and the blue bitter smoke of wood:
And radiant raindrops couching in cool flowers;
And flowers themselves, that sway through sunny hours;
Dreaming of moths that drink them under the moon;
Then, the cool kindliness of sheets, that soon
Smooth away trouble; and the rough male kiss
Of blankets; grainy wood; live hair that is
Shining and free; blue-massing clouds; the keen
Unpassioned beauty of a great machine;
The benison of hot water; furs to touch;
The good smell of old clothes; and other such --
The comfortable smell of friendly fingers,
Hair's fragrance, and the musty reek that lingers
About dead leaves and last year's ferns....
                          Dear names,
And thousand others throng to me! Royal flames;
Sweet water's dimpling laugh from tap or spring;
Holes in the ground; and voices that do sing:
Voices in laughter, too; and body's pain,
Soon turned to peace; and the deep-panting train;
Firm sands; the little dulling edge of foam
That browns and dwindles as the wave goes home;
And washen stones, gay for an hour; the cold
Graveness of iron; moist black earthen mold;
Sleep; and high places; footprints in the dew;
And oaks; and brown horse-chestnuts, glossy-new;
And new-peeled sticks; and shining pools on grass; --
All these have been my loves. And these shall pass,
Whatever passes not, in the great hour.
Nor all my passion, all my prayers, have power
To hold them with me through the gate of Death.

Exercise

Write a poem called "These I have loved."

Through the senses we penetrate through the veil of subjectivity and that which hides the world from us; it thereby becomes possible to break through to higher worlds.

Tone

One of the most neglected aspects of poetry is Tone. Because the poem is required to say much in few words, it becomes essential that indications, no matter how subtle, are included in the poem to help the reader determine the tone or feeling quality of the experience.

In speech or oral reading, the voice may serve to establish the tone, but to express emotional nuances through the little black lines on the page requires skill. Words alone do not determine meaning. Tone must be taken into consideration.

"I love you," may be meant as a statement of hate, of love, of questioning, etc. Who has not had the experience of silence from a friend to whom a letter was sent, which letter had been read in a tone altogether different from that which was meant by the writer?

Some of the ways tone may be indicated are:

1. <u>Length of the line</u>: Lines of great length in free flowing style may indicate a mood of relaxation. Short lines may create hesitant, nervous mood.

2. Use of particular <u>sounds</u>: Knowledge of the affective primal quality of sound may help the poet establish particular emotional responses.

Edgar Allen Poe made many experiments in this area. For example, he determined that the sounds, S, L, N, and AW create an atmosphere of melancholy as in "The lost Lenore." (See chapter on Sound.)

3. Use of skillful <u>imagery</u>: Imagery can establish tone without the necessity of defining an abstract rendition of emotion. For example, the following image would more readily establish the mood of the poem than the statement, "I felt terrible." "The clothing hanging in the closets reminded me of mummies I had seen hanging on hooks in the sepulchres of Guanajuato."

How different the mood becomes if one says, "The clothing hanging in the closets looked like colorful carnival marionettes."

 4. <u>Rhythm</u> is a great indicator of tone. Knowledge of the affective qualities of rhythms is essential.

 5. <u>Punctuation</u> has as its major role to aid in establishing tone. A question mark asks a question. An exclamation point emphasizes.

 6. Use of particular <u>rhyme</u> patterns can indicate joy, fear, reverence, etc.

 7. <u>Color</u> is associated with various emotional and moral experiences. By introducing certain colors, awe, piety, or passion may be expressed.

 8. <u>Metres</u> are particularly effective in establishing tone. (See chapter on metres.)

SOME FURTHER ASPECTS OF TONE

 The Greeks taught how certain soul states are associated with the God, Apollo, others with Dionysius. The quality which is associated with Apollo streams in from the periphery and tends to be connected with clarity of thought. That which is associated with Dionysius is centrifugal, originating within "the guts," so to speak -- the dark inner unconscious. It tends to be highly emotional and intense. Poems dealing with memory wherein one tends to philosophize are Apollonian, those of immediate emotional intensity, Dionysian.

Exercise

 When writing the next poems, and when you see the first version, ask yourself if what the poem wishes to express is cearly objective or highly emotional. By determining this, you bring unity into the work and chart its direction and awareness.

SOUL MOODS OR EMOTIONS

 Some of the basic soul moods include:

    solemnity
    wisdom
    piety, reverence, awe, etc.
    inwardness
    compassion, love, affection, etc.

                    insatiability
                    cleverness
                    self-assertion
                    sadness, grief, mourning, etc.
                    happiness, joy, etc.
                    despair
                    questioning
                    exclamation

   In poetic language, express the following in individual but related lines:

   You are walking on the beach at a particular time of day or night, of season, and a mood of solemnity exists. Write a line indicating this mood.

   A philosophical thought enters your mind. The next line should express this.

   A feeling of reverence or wonder enters. Express this in the third line.

   You give vent to a feeling of love in the fourth line.

   Then a great sadness overwhelms you. Express this in poetic imagery.

   This is soon turned to joy by something which occurs.

   A question arises to your lips.

   You utter an exclamation of assertion.

   You can give yourself exercises of this nature, combining different emotions. Below is an example of the above exercise and what it expresses:

In silence of slow moving priestly waters	(Solemnity)
Out of the sea they came	(Meditative piety)
Soft-footed, moving slow	
Heads bowed, eyes seeing	
And unseeing	
Speak! Stretch out your hands,	(Communication)
Say silent words	
That sound like bells in other voices,	
Through an unmoving darkness	
Always moving.	(Despair)

Oh, holy ones! Behold love's light   (Exclamation)
In its final meaning!
Now joy flies upward
and on winged feet touches the stars.   (Joy)

Arising from the waters,   (Question)
Shall we fly?

                    Aphrodite, Her Birth

          Nothing to tell,
          nothing having happened,
          this I tell of it
          it is becoming.

          of her birth
          of tides swelling
          of the wind telling

          ocean magic formed and the sea
          found limbs to smooth and draw
          in, knotting: Suddenly

          waves, quiescent to the moon
          foamed, spoke her coming
          drew themselves in

          gulls rolled
          soft on the wind
          by, everything was easy
          everything flowed
          and was slow, the season, summer

          early it was,
          dipped and made light
          of the heat but lolled
          newer and slower. Potent
          oh potent, then she, becoming,
          came is still
          Coming.

Another Exercise

    Make a list of various emotions. Human emotions are legion. Example: jealousy, nostalgia, despair, hate melancholy, vengeance, etc. Choose one of those emotions and make notes concerning how it may be expressed. Indicate color, physical manifestations, suitable comparisons, rhythm, etc.

Next, carry only a particular emotion through in a poem. It will be easier if you attempt to recall a particular strong emotional experience, and, using the stream of consciousness, write about it.

Now organize the experience into a poem, utilizing some of the techniques we have already discussed.

Exercises

1. Taking some aspect of our theme, write a long flowing line.

2. Referring to the discussion of the chapter on Sound, write several lines using particular emotions:

   <u>Example</u>: W and B: "Oh wild west wind, thou breath
   of autumn's being..."
   (Shelley)

3. Write several figures of speech and indicate what emotion they are meant to call forth.

4. From what has been discussed in the chapter on Rhythm, try to write some lines in different rhythms which establish particular moods.

5. Write several lines of exclamations.

6. Color: Write a line that calls forth the emotional reaction which the color red would call forth. Now yellow. Now blue, etc.

Give yourself further exercises of this nature.

Note how different poets have used some of the above principles in composing their work.

EXAMPLE OF A DIONYSIAN MOOD

Excerpts from *Anatomy of Prayer*

Grass

Laid is the blanket
And I, upon the tendrils of peace.
Morning rests on my shoulders.

Most gentle grasses
I have a song for thee
Most serpentine seedlings
Thou art the sweet breath blowing...
O verdant and anonymous lyre

Stroke for me
The Ballad of the Howling Man

Howl   howl   howl goes
The Howling Man
Too full of himself to speak

        My bulk is Abstract--I am your sky
        My rage is Crimson--I am your weather

I believe my conscience to be a Theory
I am your God.

Save   the Fool God--green-healer
Save the man from his howl
Green-balancer
Sustenance of cattle
Cushioner of armies

                      below ye lies

The incomprehensible mutterings
Of Minerals
Omni-dark and jutting sliced silences
                      and above ye
My world of blood and
Sour ballads.
Song is sung and
This is what is falling:
Atomic wastes dandruffed and poison
Prehistoric trees and the spit of
Cats. Tears of an audience
Raving in the
Theatre of the Sun.

O blessed carpet
To thy moistness they shall all return worms.
Leaden subjects in a darkness
Ruled by worms.

62

EXAMPLE OF A POEM WITH APOLLONIAN DIRECTION

Clouds

As dark as purple,
as bright as orange into crimson,
as delicate as yellow,
their sudden bodies gather on the morning
and for the little time I watch them -
of things that fly, the loveliest are these.

They gather on the walls of morning,
or for the blue distances above them they rise
they all of them rise and are scattered
and in the world they want
how small they are
and everywhere I look - how white.
Though when the wind
too roughly touches them -
then from their bodies
that are made of only cloud,
feathers of color drift down.

EXAMPLE OF A POEM IN WHICH COLOR ESTABLISHES A MOOD

       Blue Clothes

   would be fine, if I were a bird
water
the wind.

Clothes that shut my meager, naked body in,
such blue
      for the sea
a dream, a moment
          of the sea...

Forced into my heart, the blood
flows, pain-
ful.
Red tag, square and stiff:
to be free of you
I might gladly die,
gladly become scattered ash.

Through the black night yearning for dawn,
if only the tears falling from expectant eyes
might reflect just once
the lucence of the morning-glory,
and brighten with sun's illumination;

if only to stand for a moment
in sunlight pouring down
from blue skies that in every dream
pierce the black clouds
open, gladly,
imprisoned in these blue clothes

I would gladly die
if that were to be real,
this moment,
and not hidden
till the very end.

EXAMPLE OF AN EMOTION CARRIED THROUGH A POEM: DESPAIR

In a perpetual dusk

In a perpetual
   dusk cumulous wings of smog
      reeking of sulphur and charred hearts
      writhe in obligato hover
   through the phantom of your strained
face etched with tombstone crags
of the shattered mirrors
   of my house wherein your stark
      eyes are grotesquely multiplied
      No wind shakes free the dead branches
   of this cemetery where
uselessly I water
rusty metal flowers
   you have planted Once again
      I begin the long crawl uphill
      who believed forever vanquished
   the albatross of despair
   seeking resurrection
on the opposite side
   of the canvas of the green
      crucified flesh and the smashed feet
      Bowed beneath transformed illusion
   strangled by grey gravity
the heart dessicated
what use to know Light IS?
   Come distilled gold dust flow through
      the ventricles and auricles
      through my skull may an aura rise
   dissolve as salt in water
these dense vapors shaking
tree skeletons to bud
   piercing the fear-hardened soil
      to flower. Come butterflies, birds
      A clear breeze The trees speak I hear
   as if under water curved
chords of the Angelus.

Sound Structure

Ancient wisdom teaches much concerning the primal quality of sound. Some scholars, from ancient times to the present, have believed that the word has a divine origin, and that if one was in tune with an experience, the sounds basic to that experience would emerge. The Book of Genesis speaks of an original language, which was fractured when humans tried to be as gods, so that people could no longer understand each other. The aim then of evolution was to evolve in consciousness to that state when human beings will again understand the primal language.

If one believes this, then as a poet, one may play a major role in that worthy task.

Speech scholars have proven that sound has an affective quality; that is, that specific sounds call forth specific emotions. Major writers at all times have known this. In the *Atharva Veda* of ancient India there is a collection of curses, charms, and prayers, the sounds of which could work magic. It is said that certain sounds heal, others can kill. Some ancient armies used curses on the battlefield as a destroyer of morale. Edgar Allan Poe was a great student of primal sound and wrote many books, little known today, on the affective quality of sound. He came to the conclusion for example, that sounds like m, n, aw, o, b, l, w, ier, s could evoke melancholy and mystery: "The Lost Lenore...": "The dim lake of Ober...", "The misty mid region of Wier."

Shakespeare was the master of sound structure. In his works, one can leave off the initial consonants of words in a single line, and note a progression of vowels which integrate the emotion conveyed.

Sound poems have been written which, though non-objective, nevertheless evoke experience: "Jabberwocky" in *Alice in Wonderland*, Christian Morganstern's "The Great Lalula," the sound poems of Hugo Ball and Kurt Schwitters, the great poem of James Joyce, *Ulysses*, and others.

Mantrams or verses for meditation have at all times exerted great power, and no one can deny the effect of many nursery rhymes which make non-sense.

The poet must learn as much as possible in the realm of affective sound.

From various language scholars, we may derive the following information:

<u>Consonants</u> are form giving; they structure the word and make articulation possible. They are connected with thought.

<u>Vowels</u> give the emotional quality of the word.

Rudolf Steiner, the Austrian philosopher, has indicated the following primal characteristics of sounds:

<u>Consonants</u>

b: a protective embracing quality
k: a cutting, clipped effect
d: pointing or calming
f: an intellectual sound: "Know that I know!"
g: clearing a barrier so that the self may assert itself
h: freeing oneself from that which hems in
l: a water sound, healing. It is like a fountain, ever renewed
m: evolved consciousness: m moves out into the world, feeling its way forward
n: One touches objects and gets to know them, but one does not grab or possess
p: a sign of beauty and pride
r: r rolls. It is an air sound. Without air there is no speech. A dynamic sound of movement.
s: a sound that can heal, quiet, or kill if it hisses like the sound of a snake
t: a sound of knowledge and definition
v: a sound that pushes forward like the horns of a ram, or waves of the ocean; a dynamic sound
w: a water sound: (Some scholars believe WAH was the first word.)
z: or ts,: a sound of balance and spiraling upward

<u>Vowels</u>

ah: sound of wonder, love
e: (pronounced as ee) sound of the ego, of the intellect. At the other exteme, it closes one to the world.
o: (pronounced oh) embracing and going out to the world

u: on the one hand, a cool sound, a sound in awe and
    fear; on the other, a gathering oneself together.
ei: (pronounced as in stay) separating oneself: holding
    oneself together

The dipthongs are combinations of the above.

Rhyme and appeal to the sense of hearing as we have already noted, are connected with sound structure.

Sound structure may indeed be the most important aspect of poetry.

When writing the first notes for a poem, you will already note that certain sounds prevail. In the artistic fashioning of the poem, you may then work with those and find words which express in sound the tone you wish to convey.

Exercises

Write a poem in which one of the above sounds plays a major role.

B

be
be B
born
body
bear
build
beget
borne
becalm
behold!
become...

to gather in
to   make whole
                    - quiet
        inwardness

to awaken
   and calm
to   move
the   world
person in the
     inner light of
          the   Sun

below   above   encircling   our sphere   the horizon
                                    this   is B B B

Write a sound poem which has no recognizable complete words, but makes its effect with the inclusion of specific sounds or combinations of parts of words.

Jabberwocky

'Twas brillig, and the slithy toves
  Did gyre and gimble in the wabe:
All mimsy were the borogoves,
  And the mome raths outgrabe.

"Beware the Jabberwock, my son!
  The jaws that bite, the claws that catch!
Beware the Jubjub bird, and shun
  The frumious Bandersnatch!"

He took his vorpal sword in hand;
  Long time the manxome foe he sought--
So rested he by the Tumtum tree,
  And stood awhile in thought.

And, as in uffish thought he stood,
  The Jabberwock, with eyes of flame,
Came whiffling through the tulgey wood,
  And burbled as it came!

One, two! One, two! And through and through
  The vorpal blade went snicker-snack!
He left it dead, and with its head
  He went galumphing back.

"And hast thou slaim the Jabberwock?
  Come to my arms, my beamish boy!
O frabjous day! Callooh, Callay!"
  He chortled in his joy.

'Twas brillig, and the slithy toves
  Did gyre and gimble in the wabe:
All mimsy were the borogoves,
  And the mome raths outgrabe.

A SOUND POEM

The great Lalula

Kroklokwafzi? Semememi!
Seickrontro - prafiplo:
Bifzi, bafzi, hulalemi:
quasti basti bo...

Hontaruru micromente
zasku zes ru ru?
Entrepente, leiolente
Klekwapufzi lu?
lalu lalu lalu lalu la!

Simarar kos malzipempu
silzuzankunkrei(;) !
Marjomar dos: Quempu Lempu
Siri Suri Sei;!
Lalu lalu lalu lalu la!

WORD PLAY

Washington Square

Here begins all indelving
Childmens drib into the brainit
And enter the Nervit spirs
Treeleaves lighten and shimmering shake
The hoary greenhair on oldbeauty ruins
As in the Caracalla one listiencing to Traviata
Awarens ancient kingleads at their baths
Lucent beyond the costumed actsingers
So I dreamwaning around the fountain in Washington
    Square
Dress myself in nostalgrevs
When the furious winds on Octember loved me
And stars were personal and starp
And all wondawes and marvtransformings were before us
Now these are only rememoires
    And the seageons are dead.

Rhyme

Rhyming is concerned with the combinations of sounds which are similar. Ancient teachers knew that certain sound combinations were capable of reaching deeply into the soul. They often used rhymed verses as a kind of magic which could transform behavior. All good poems in fact, perpetuate a kind of magic which is capable of awakening feelings and thoughts, and of moving to action.

The reading of poetry should enrich, not waste time. Therefore he who writes has the responsibility of not adding to the clutter of dead matter which crowds the shelves of libraries.

To know rhyming intimately, with its intricacies and many facets, is to be able to enrich the poetic experience.

Those who know little about poetry believe that rhyme means only one thing: end rhyme: that is, the rhyming of two sressed syllables at the end of a couplet.

The sky is blue
And I love you.

If rhyme however is defined as the combination of similar sounds, infinite possibilities exist, and subtle poems of multiple meaning may be created. The great poets of all time have always known this. Shakespeare was one of the greatest geniuses of rhyme. One learns in school that most of the plays are written in blank verse which implies a line of five beats and no rhyme. The truth is that Shakespeare's plays are filled with all manner of ingenious rhymes. Emily Dickinson, whose poems remained unpublished while she lived because it was believed she was a poor craftsman, actually was a genius of "off-rhymes." Poets today are fortunate in that they may explore an infinite number of techniques without censure.

Using many-faceted rhyme is to become skilled in verbal texture. To become aware of this, even as a reader, is to experience the skill of the artist at work.

Beware of forced rhyme. This means to rhyme words merely for the sake of the rhyme, and at the risk of destroying the tone. Even the most inexperienced reader detects forced rhyme. Rhyme lifts the expression out of the banality of prose into incantation.

It was in the Middle Ages that poets began to use rhyme as we know it today. The following are examples of the innumerable rhyme possibilities:

1. End-Rhyme: rhyme of the final stressed syllables:

> I think that I shall never see
> A poem as lovely as a tree ...
>
> *from Trees* by Joyce Kilmer

2. Half-rhyme called assonance: a similar resonance in the last stressed syllables of two or more words:

> Love's stricken "why"
> It's all that love can speak
> Built of but just a syllable
> The hugest hearts that break.
>
> *Love's stricken "Why"* by Emily Dickinson

3. Rhyme of initial consonants in a single line:

> I caught this morning morning's minion...
>
> *from The Windhover* by Gerard Manley Hopkins

4. Internal rhyme: rhymes which move throughout the poem:

> We are leaning
> toward the perpendicular shades
> the trees make. Greening
> single spear of hyacinth
> from earth-hilt. We leave
> the women talking secretly
> to their dogs, feeding
> pigeons whose names are all Peter...
>
> *from Spring* by Daisy Aldan

72

5. <u>Full rhyme</u>: vowels and consonants rhyme:

    Roll on, thou deep and dark blue Ocean - <u>roll</u>!
    Ten thousand fleets sweep over thee in vain;
    Man marks the earth with ruin; his cont<u>rol</u>
    Stops with the shore...

6. <u>Consonant rhyme</u>: The consonants rhyme, not the vowels.

    The stars rose <u>late</u>
    and shed a <u>light</u>
    as if the <u>guest</u>
    had been a <u>ghost</u>...

7. <u>Rhyming the unstressed syllables</u> (called feminine rhyme):

    Nobody comes to give him his rum but the
    Rim of the sky hippopotamus - glum
    Enhances the chances to bless with a benison
    Alfred Lord Tenny<u>son</u> crossing the bar laid
    With cold vegetat<u>ion</u> from pale deputat<u>ion</u>...

              from *Sir Beelzebub* by
                 Edith Sitwell

8. <u>Rhyming of the last word of one line with the first word of the next line</u>:

    The wounds of the <u>dark</u>
    <u>hark</u> back to the past...

9. <u>Rhyming a one-syllable word with the last syllable of another word</u>:

    Christ that each day, each night, nails there, have mercy
      on <u>us</u> -
    On Dives and on <u>Lazarus</u>:...

              from *Still Falls the Rain* by
                 Edith Sitwell

10. <u>Rhyming of the last consonant only</u>:

    The grass divides as with a comb,
    A spotted shaft is <u>seen</u>;
    And then it closes at your feet
    And opens further <u>on</u>.
              Emily Dickinson

(This is also an example of assonance.)

11. One can rhyme in such a way that the rhyme is <u>not obvious</u>: The line continues onto the following line and does not end the thought at the end of the line. Robert Browning was a master of this.

> That's my last Duchess painted on the <u>wall</u>
> Looking as if she were alive. I <u>call</u>
> That piece a wonder now. Fra Pandolf's <u>hands</u>
> Worked busily a day, and there she <u>stands</u>.

> from *My Last Duchess* by Robert Browning

Rhyme helps structure the poem. However, structure must be used to enhance the poem, not imposed on it.

<u>Paired rhyme</u>: aa bb

> What is to come, we know not. But we know
> That what has been was good -- was good to show,
>   Better to hide, and best of all to bear.
> We are the masters of the days that were....

> from *What is to come* by W. B. Henley

<u>Crossed rhyme</u>: abcb

> The splendor falls on castle walls
>   And snowy summits old in story:
> The long light shakes across the lakes
>   And the wild cataract leaps in glory.

> from *Blow, Bugle, Blow* by Alfred Lord Tennyson

<u>Enclosed rhyme</u>: abba

> O Earth, lie heavily upon her eyes:
> Seal her sweet eyes weary of watching. Earth;
> Lie close around her; leave no room for mirth
> With its harsh laughter, nor for sound of sighs.

> from *Rest* by Christina Rosseti

Exercise

Write a poem on some aspect of "Tides" using a definite rhyme scheme. Try to study your first version and notes, and discover what rhymes already exist therein. Use the meditated stream of consciousness if you have difficulty beginning. Or take a poem you have already written and restructure it.

The possibilities are legion. The ingenuity of the poet is all.

Find and indicate the rhymes in the following poem. See if you can identify them by name or type:

> The Windhover:
>
> To Christ our Lord

I CAUGHT this morning morning's minion, king-
  dom of daylight's dauphin, dapple-dawn-drawn Falcon, in
    his riding
Of the rolling level underneath him steady air, and striding
High there, how he rung upon the rein of a wimpling wing
In his ecstasy! then off, off forth on swing,
  As a skate's heel sweeps smooth on a bow-bend; the hurl
    and gliding
Rebuffed the big wind. My heart in hiding
Stirred for a bird, -- the achieve of, the mastery of the thing!

Brute beauty and valour and act, oh, air, pride, plume, here
  Buckle! AND the fire that breaks from thee then, a billion
Times told lovelier, more dangerous, O my chevalier!

No wonder of it: sheer plod makes plough down sillion
Shine, and blue-bleak embers, ah my dear,
  Fall, gall themselves, and gash gold-vermilion.

                        Gerard Manley Hopkins

POEM WITH MANY SLANT AND INTERNAL RHYMES
Relic

Like seaweed the white foot
lies on the sand
to be swallowed up
by the first high tide

The foam moans low
(it moans low)
and the real seaweed like jelly fish moves
nearer the foot
where now the water swirls
and toils to make more white
that pure bone

That foot
near the sea tide
must lie
dismembered
without color
with form
primordial, animal
soon to be fleshless
entire

A white clean fragment
of a man
once encumbered
by total flesh by arm
by woman
by ship's chores

by war
by a death
eccentric:

irrelevant now the womb leanings
that male body
that fatherhood
that Vietnamese whore.

Clean bone
washed by sea tide
relic

--coming from the shore
that limb once managed well
once *walked*
walked
like Him who *walked* the waves.

Structure

The Poet's eye in a fine frenzy rolling
Doth glance from heaven to earth, from earth to heaven
And as imagination bodies forth
The form of things unknown, the poet's pen
Turns them to shapes, and gives to airy nothing
A local habitation and a name.

                          Theseus in *Love's Labour Lost*
                             by William Shakespeare

Many people who manifest talent express themselves freely, leaving form or structure to chance. Some do this out of ignorance, others believe that any haphazard scratchings on paper are poems. However, as the body cannot exist without the inner skeleton, no work of art can be formless. The amateur occasionally may produce a fine poem accidentally, but an experienced reader can easily detect the work of the inexperienced writer. As with the body's skeleton, the inner structure of the poem must be unobtrusive. Poems which seem most free are based on the most careful structure. True freedom is not anarchy, as some moderns imply, but results from diligent discipline. This is true of art as well as of all other life activities.

Characteristics of Structure

1. <u>Placement</u> of the poem on the page: the poem is also a visual experience and how or where the poem is placed adds or detracts from meaning or tone.

2. <u>Metre</u>: The number of beats to a line; or <u>Syllabic</u> structure, which is based on the number of syllables in each line.

3. <u>Line Length</u>.

4. <u>Typefaces</u>: Use of capital or small letters (called upper case and lower case); use of bold or normal typefaces.

5. <u>Stanza</u> arrangement.

6. <u>Arrangement</u> and <u>spacing</u> of lines.

7. <u>Type of poem</u> may determine the structure: epic, lyric, narrative, dramatic, etc. Classic structures have particular patterns: sonnets, haikus, villanelles, ballads, etc. Contemporary poems also have determined forms: free verse, concrete poems, etc.

Every art has laws according to which it is structured. In our time form is no longer determined by exterior considerations as it was in the classic and neoclassic periods. The individual vision of the artist determines form today. True poetry makes strong demands. A poem is a living organism and must have equilibrium. This does not imply that it cannot express experiences of dissonance. It is not merely a question of harmonious form, but of a form which is capable of also embodying dissonance.

Many people begin well, but then employ too many images or too many words and thus confuse the essential. Others omit too much. Or they do not come to a conclusion. The poem lacks either head or feet, so to speak. Sometimes the ideas are praiseworthy, but clarity is absent because an appropriate form has not been found. The true artist is not he who has a sudden inspiration, but he who with perseverence molds and forms in order to come to a defined revelation of his vision.

Form

There exist Classical forms and Contemporary forms.

1. <u>Classical</u>: The poet attempts to embody his idea in a form which is determined by convention, exteriorly. Here, there is a danger that the poem will be forced into a structure which may be arbitrary and not integral to the experience, the form of a straitjacket. Classical forms have rigid models: the ends of lines exist in distinct places; metres are determined by exterior rules for special types; there are determined classical rhythms; and the design and pattern may be arbitrarily determined.

2. <u>Contemporary</u>: In our time, the possibilities of form are infinite. It depends entirely on the ingenuity of the poet, the individual artist. The poem itself determines the form it needs. This does not mean it must be left to chance: one must learn to listen and feel what the poem wishes to express, and how it gives hints of the form it requires. Experience teaches the poet to recognize incor-

rect structures. It may be compared to the situation in which a composer is able to hear a false note in a composition. Every single poem today may have its own structure, just as leaves from the same tree are individual, even though it requires subtle vision to detect this.

Here also there are dangers to be avoided. Many modern poets would throw all form out the window. This would be similar to the wish of anarchists to destroy the whole world, thereby forgetting that every step in mankind's evolution contains past and future in it, and that one may not be separated from the other. Classical forms are easily imitated, but the flowing forms of contemporary poetry are qualitative, thus difficult to imitate. The question arises: how does one achieve such a free-flowing form without predetermined metrical beats? This may be achieved by syllabic structure.

Syllabic Structure

Instead of counting the beats of stressed and unstressed syllables, one counts the number of syllables in each line, and patterns the poem accordingly. The English language lends itself to syllabic structure because it is a language which flows, having had its origin in a country which was surrounded by flowing waters.

POEM IN SYLLABIC STRUCTURE

Out of Her Exile

Out of her exile
out of the blurred webs of her dream
out of the captive shroud of stony death
she emerges into a drift of light
which illumines the flowering fruit trees,
their benevolent gestures.

Star rays resonate
in revolving, reaching toward her
who molds herself forth to the encounter.
After long gestation in impotence,
she survives the <u>major</u> implorings, <u>minor</u>
retreats, dissonant defeats.

Weaving a cosmic
geometry in curves, spirals
and angles of the intoned Word, having
trusted its constancy among confusions,
one incredible morning, she rises,
stirs, chooses, becomes a world.

Exercise

Consciously employ syllabic structure in a poem based on our theme, thereby also determining the pattern of stanzas as exemplified in the above poem.

Spacing

In poetry, every space is important. As in music, essence lies in the silences between the words. In classical poetry, stanza forms were predetermined and spaces had a regularity. The poem was placed in the center of the page with a kind of open frame around it. Contemporary poetry accepts a great freedom in spacing, and thereby the possibilities of the poem as a vehicle of multiple meaning and spiritual experience have been enhanced.

The great French poet, Stephane Mallarmé, was an innovator and introduced many new patterns of spacing: spacing between words to take the place of punctuation, between phrases, even between letters. He stated that he "wished to let the light in." Here is an example from his *Un Coup De Des* (A Throw of the Dice).

    Excerpt from *A Throw of the Dice*
        by Stephane Mallarmé

rather
    than
        as the old madman
           play the game
      in behalf of the waves

                            one   surges over the chief
                                flows over the submissive
                              graybeard

                direct shipwreck   of the man
                            without a ship

Another example of a poem where spacing and consonant structure play important parts:

Mercurial Pitching Sunbeams

```
mercurial
        pitching
                sunbeams
                        emerge as gulls
                                grouped by the wind
                                                -how do fragile
                                                    wings
                        endure          the wind's
                                            thrust              ?
```

Spacing used to enhance the concept of snow falling:

White Weather

```
            In January aviaries

         of a very very day

             white is

                    white is
                white is
                        very feathered

            white-weathered

    a

         very

            poem.
```

Characteristics of Spacing

    1. Spacing may denote a pause, a breath as a comma denotes a breath.

    2. Spacing may be used to enhance and emphasize the meaning of a particular word. Most people these days read quickly, hardly recognizing the special significance of individual words. By placing space before that word which one wishes to stress, the reader is forced to pause and to note it. The <u>living</u> quality of the word is returned to what had become a dead abstrac-

tion. In this way also, the reader becomes an active participant in the poem.

    3. A space may take the place of punctuation. Most people do not realize that rules of punctuation are fairly recent. In expository writing punctuation correctly used is essential for immediate communication, but in poetry, it is the poet who determines how he wishes to employ punctuation <u>creatively</u>. Of course, arbitrary omission of punctuation or omission through ignorance is inexcusable. One should have a good reason for every omission of colon, comma, exclamation point, etc., -- or their inclusion.

    4. Spacing may be used to focus attention. It is important to be attentive to the last word in each line, for ending a line at a particular word means there will be a pause before the eyes reach the first word of the succeeding line, which then becomes important through its placement.

    5. Spacing between stanzas is important. This space, smaller or larger, adds to the context.

    6. Spacing may change the pace of the poem. The breath stream of the reader is affected and a slow or fast pace may alter tone or meaning.

```
       A POEM WHERE SPACING IS USED TO SLOW UP
         THE PACE AND BRING GREATER FOCUS
                 ON PARTICULAR WORDS

                    The Wave


The wave is confronted by moonlight or
                      by              sun-
                            light

They                  meet
      in              my                    eye.


My 'I' weaves the dark
           water
           with              gold
                 the dark
           water
           with                    running quicksilver
       in                                         light of
my          thinking
           whose
           Word                                       calls
                their                                       name.


Man
must reveal the wave for
            the       sake of
            the wave for
            the       sake of
Man.
```

Stanza Forms

    Novels are divided into chapters. Plays have scenes and acts. The divisions in poetry are called <u>stanzas</u>.

Stanza Forms with Defined Patterns

1. <u>Couplet</u>: Two matching lines of verse.

EXAMPLE

If You

If you were going to get a pet
what kind of animal would you get.

A soft bodied dog, a hen –
feathers and fur to begin it again.

When the sun goes down and it gets dark
I saw an animal in a park.

Bring it home, to give it to you.
I have seen animals break in two.

You were hoping for something soft
and loyal and clean and wondrously careful –

a form of otherwise vicious habit
can have long ears and be called a rabbit.

Dead. Died. Will die. Want.
Morning midnight. I asked you,
if you were going to get a pet
what kind of animal would you get.

85

2. <u>Tercet</u>: Three rhyming lines.

EXAMPLE

Upon Julia's Clothes

Whenas in silks my Julia goes
Then, then (methinks) how sweetly flows
That liquefaction of her clothes.

Next, when I cast mine eyes and see
That brave vibration each way free;
O how that glittering taketh me.

3. <u>Quatrain</u>: Four lines which may be rhymed in a variety of ways: abab, abba, etc.

EXAMPLE

from *The Douglas Tragedy*

Lady Margaret was on a milk-white steed,
  Lord William was on a gray,
A buglet-horn hung down by his side,
  And swiftly they rode away.

4. <u>Quintet</u>: Five lines which may be variously rhymed: ababb, etc.

EXAMPLE

The Bourne

Underneath the growing grass,
  Underneath the living flowers,
  Deeper than the sound of showers;
  There we shall not count the hours
By the shadows as they pass.

Youth and health will be but vain,
  Beauty reckoned of no worth:
  There a very little girth
  Can hold round what once the earth
Seemed too narrow to contain.

5. <u>Sestet</u>: Six lines which may be rhymed in many ways: aaabab, etc.

EXAMPLE

from *The Blessed Damozel*

    The blessed damozel leaned out
      From the gold bar of Heaven;
    Her eyes were deeper than the depth
      Of waters stilled at even;
    She had three lilies in her hand,
      And the stars in her hair were seven.

6. <u>Septet</u>: Known as <u>rime royal</u>; variously rhymed lines: ababbcc, etc.

EXAMPLE

from *A Leave-Taking*

    Let us go hence my songs, she will not hear:
    Let us go hence together, without fear.
    Keep silence now for singing time is over
    And over all old things and all things dear.
    She loves not you nor me as all we love her.
    Yeah, though we sang as angels in her ear,
    She would not hear.

7. <u>Octave</u>: Eight lines which may be combinations of the above, aaabcccg, etc.

EXAMPLE

from *Don Juan*

Soft hour! which wakes the wish and melts the heart
    Of those who sail the seas, on the first day
When they from their sweet friends are torn apart;
    Or fills with love the pilgrim on his way
As the far bell of vesper makes him start,
    Seeming to weep the dying day's decay;
Is this a fancy which our reason scorns?
Ah! surely nothing dies but something mourns.

8. <u>Spenserian stanza</u>: Nine lines rhymed as follows: ababbcbcc

EXAMPLE

from *The Eve of St. Agnes*

  A casement high and triple-arched there was,
  All garlanded with carven imageries,
Of fruits and flowers, and bunches of knot-grass,
  And diamonded with panes of quaint device,
  Innumerable of stains and splendid dyes,
  As are the tiger-moth's deep-damasked wings;
  And in the midst, 'mong thousand heraldries,
  And twilight saints, and dim emblazonings,
A shielded scutcheon blushed with blood of queens and kings.

Some Classical Forms

The Sonnet

    Sonnets are built on fourteen lines, each line composed of ten syllables in iambic metre which makes ten beats to a line. The first eight lines are called the octave, the second, the sestet. There are three types of sonnet:

    1. The Petrarchian: rhymed as follows: abbaabba cdceed

    2. The Shakespearian: rhymed as follows: ababcdcd efefgg

    3. The Miltonic: rhymed as follows: abbaabbacdcdcd

In the Miltonic sonnet, the sestet is not separate from the octave.

EXAMPLE: A SONNET BY SHAKESPEARE

XXIX

When in disgrace with Fortune and men's eyes,
I all alone beweep my outcast state,
And trouble deaf heaven with my bootless cries,
And look upon myself, and curse my fate,
Wishing me like to one more rich in hope,
Featur'd like him, like him with friends
    possess'd,
Desiring this man's art, and that man's scope,
With what I most enjoy contented least;
Yet in these thoughts myself almost despising,
Haply I think on thee, and then my state,
Like to the lark at break of day arising
From sullen earth, sings hymns at heaven's gate;
  For thy sweet love remember'd such wealth
     brings
  That then I scorn to change my state with
     kings.

The Ballade

    The ballade has three stanzas of eight lines each, and a half stanza of four lines called the envoy. The rhymes of the first stanza are arranged thus: ababbcbc. The envoy would then be bcbc. This is repeated in all the stanzas. There is a <u>refrain</u>; a line which ends every stanza is repeated in each stanza and ends the envoy. Thus:

    a b a b b c b c

    a b a b b c b c

    a b a b b c b c

    Envoy: b c b c

EXAMPLE

A Ballade of Dreamland

I hid my heart in a nest of roses,
    Out of the sun's way, hidden apart;
In a softer bed than the soft white snow's is,
    Under the roses I hid my heart.
    Why would it sleep not? Why should it start,
When never a leaf of the rose-tree stirred?
    What made sleep flutter his wings and part?
Only the song of a secret bird.

Lie still, I said, for the wind's song closes
    And mild leaves muffle the keen sun's dart;
Lie still, for the wind on the warm seas dozes,
    And the wind is unquieter yet than thou art.
    Does a thought in thee still as a thorn's wound smart?
Does the fang still fret thee of hope deferred?
    What birds the lips of thy sleep dispart?
Only the song of a secret bird.

The green land's name that a charm encloses,
    It never was writ in the traveller's chart,
And sweet on its trees as the fruit that grows is;
    It never was sold in the merchant's mart.
    The swallows of dreams through its dim fields dart,
And sleep's are the tunes in its tree-tops heard;
    No hound's note wakens the wildwood hart,
Only the song of a secret bird.

ENVOY

In the world of dreams I have chosen my part,
    To sleep for a season and hear no word
Of true love's truth or of light love's art,
    Only the song of a secret bird.

The Rondeau

    A poem of thirteen lines built on only two rhymes, the refrain being a repetition of the first part of the first line. If x represents the refrain, the rhyme scheme would be as follows:

```
a a b b a
a a b x
a a b b a x
```

EXAMPLE

Rondeau

Let us be drunk, and for a while forget
Forget, and ceasing even from regret
Live without reason and despite of rhyme,
As in a dream preposterous and sublime,
Where place and hour and means for once
   are met.

Where is the use of effort? Love and debt
And disappointment have us in a net.
Let us break out, and taste the morning prime...
   Let us be drunk.

In vain our little hour we strut and fret,
And mouth our wretched parts as for a bet.
We cannot please the tragicaster Time.
To gain the crystal sphere, the silver clime.
Where Sympathy sits dimpling on us yet.
   Let us be drunk!

The Villanelle

This old form has become popular with contemporary poets, and recently a volume of their villanelles has appeared. The villanelle is composed of five three-line stanzas and a concluding stanza of four lines, each stanza ending with an alternating line of the first verse. Both of these lines appear together in the last stanza as a concluding couplet. Only two rhymes are permitted throughout. Thus: a1 b a2 a b a1 a b a2 a b a1 a b a2 a b a1 a2

EXAMPLE

Do Not Go Gentle into That Good Night

Do not go gentle into that good night.
Old age should burn and rave at close of day;
Rage, rage against the dying of the light.

Though wise men at their end know dark is right,
Because their words had forked no lightning they
Do not go gentle into that good night.

91

Good men, the last wave by, crying how bright
Their frail deeds might have danced in a green bay,
Rage, rage against the dying of the light.

Wild men who caught and sang the sun in flight,
And learn, too late, they grieved it on its way.
Do not go gentle into that good night.

Grave men, near death, who see with blinding sight
Blind eyes could blaze like meteors and be gay,
Rage, rage against the dying of the light.

And you, my father, there on the sad height,
Curse, bless, me now with your fierce tears, I pray.
Do not go gentle into that good night.
Rage, rage against the dying of the light.

The Ode

Derived from the Greek word meaning "Song," the ode was usually a stately elaborate verse, often chanted by two sets of singers, one intoning the *Strophe*, the other, the *Antistrophe*. As time went on, the classic ode gave way to many loose transformations, until in the present day, any extended, richly elaborated poem whose length and stanza pattern are unpredictable may be called an ode.

EXAMPLES

A Modern Ode

Ode to Willem DeKooning

1.
Beyond the sunrise
where the black begins
                      an enormous city
                      is sending up its shutters

and just before the last lapse of nerve which I am already sorry for,
that friends describe as "just this once" in a temporary hell, I hope

I try to seize upon greatness
which is available to me
                      through generosity and
                      lavishness of spirit, yours
not to be inimitably weak
and picturesque, my self

                        but to be standing clearly
                        alone in the orange wind

while our days tumble and rant through Gotham and the Easter narrows
and I have not the courage to convict myself of cowardice or care

for now a long history slinks over the sill, of patent absurdities
and the fathomless miseries of a small person upset by personality

and I look to the flags
in your eyes as they go up
                        on the enormous walls
                        as the brave must always ascend

into the air, always the musts
like banderillas dangling

and jingling jewel-like amidst the red drops on the shoulders of men
who lead us not forward or backward, but on as we must go on

                        out into the mesmerized world
                        of inanimate voices like traffic
noises, hewing a clearing
in the crowded abyss of the West

2.

            Stars of all passing sights,
            language, thought and reality,
            "I am assuming that one knows
            what it is to be ashamed"
            and that the light we seek
            is broad and pure, not winking
            and that the evil inside us
            now and then strolls into a field
            and sits down like a forgotten rock
            while we walk on to a horizon
            line that's beautifully keen,
            precarious and doesn't sag
            beneath our variable weight

            In this dawn as in the first
            it's the Homeric rose, its scent
            that leads us up the rocky path
            into the pass where death
            can disappear or where the face
            of future senses may appear
            in a white night that opens
            after the embattled hours of day

            And the wind tears up the rose
            fountains of prehistoric light
            falling upon the blinded heroes
            who did not see enough or were not
            mad enough or felt too little
            when the blood began to pour down
            the rocky slopes into pink seas

3.

Dawn must always recur
                        to blot out stars and the terrible systems
of belief
        Dawn, which dries out the web so the wind can blow it
            spider and all, away
Dawn,
        erasing blindness from an eye inflamed,
                                            reaching for its
morning cigarette in Promethean inflection
                                        after the blames
and desparate conclusions of the dark
                                    where messages were intercepted
by an ignorant horde of thoughts
                            and all simplicities perished in desire
A bus crashes into a milk truck
                            and the girl goes skating up the avenue
with streaming hair
                roaring through fluttering newspapers
and their Athenian contradictions
                                for democracy is joined
with stunning collapsible savages, all natural and relaxed and free

as the day zooms into space and only darkness lights our lives,
with few flags flaming, imperishable courage and the gentle will
which is the individual dawn of genius rising from its bed

"maybe they're wounds, but maybe they are rubies"
                                            each painful as a sun

A Pastoral

Perhaps no vice endears me to the showboat,
Whose license permeates our deep south.
The shows are simple, not yet easy, with handsome
And toy horns trying tried and true melodies.
Silently, that vice might speak from the shade:
"Your capers have misdirected all your animals."

But, hating and laughing, risen with animals,
Who is denied admission to the showboat?
Nevertheless, because of tomorrow's shade
The lad intends to file with the green deep south.
His ankles seek the temple melodies.
His mischief stirs the rocks and keeps them handsome.

The next day, finding him less handsome,
They side with the foreseeing of animals.
From the corral the melodies
Begin to flow, teaching the showboat
(Thick is the tambour, oversold the deep south)
What flowers to press back into shade.

My affairs wrapped in shade,
My mouse-colored head shall mobilize that handsome
Energetic enemy of the deep south.
Lately worms have pestered the animals.
Alarmed at our actions, a glittering showboat
Fled from the glade of supposed melodies.

And no more in our society living melodies
Break forth under the little or no shade.
The days are guarded. A miserable showboat
Plies back and forth between the handsome
Rocks, unwatched by animals
Whose glistening breath wakens forgetfulness of the deep south.

Truly the lesson of the deep south
Is how to avoid lingering beyond melodies
That cleave to the heart before it learns what animals
Strangers are. Knowing shade
Is their apology, let us never excuse handsome
Terror, the crook'd finger of a disappearing showboat.

The psalmist thought the deep south a wonderful showboat
And to the animals he met in the shade
Said, "You are my melodies, and you are handsome."

Blank Verse

Blank verse is any unrhymed verse in iambic pentameter.

from *The Death Experience of Manes*

NADHIRA:
The purple which you wear would sore oppress me,
   apotheosis of all shades of heaven.
The blue, intensified, begins to glow,
and gold turns flame. Wedded within a heart,
which is not sanctified by godly light,
blood turns to fire and consumes all life;
and he who fears the ember, puts it out,
founders in ashes, scatters to the wind.

MANES:
O human beings, give the gods your love.

NADHIRA:
O godly beings, give to men your light.

The Haiku

The Haiku originated in Japan where every year a haiku day is celebrated and prizes are awarded for the most outstanding haiku. There are seventeen syllables in a haiku, arranged as follows:

5
7
5

EXAMPLE

The falling flower
I saw drift back to the branch
Was a butterfly.

Three Basic Forms of Poetry

There are three basic forms in poetry: the Lyric, the Epic, and the Dramatic.

1. Lyric

Usually lyrics are short poems expressing emotion. The word is derived from the musical instrument, the lyre, which was used by minstrels and bards to accompany the songs they composed and sang as they travelled from town to town.

EXAMPLE

Out of the Sleeping Deep

Out of the sleeping deep rise surgings of grief shadows
    Before is not   all is a vast present with urgings to weep
        at the cry of a tern over the marsh meadows

The storm has thrown up orange oranges unfaded and green seaweed
    White and blue masts to be held aloft leaning with wind
        ragged but trembling with renewal of the long imprisoned

And jagged logs which grief has worn into the form of birds
    Yellow grapefruits heavy and round as harvest moons
        and spongy as encloistered longings

Old toys filled with the delicate moan
    of childhood which woke to your words
        and drowned weighted with tearful sand

A chair skeleton curled on a winter beach and calling uncoils
    fragility of phantasmal fantasies. For all loves are first love
        and each meeting a new losing a new yearning

Your coming now as before after a storm at sea is not Chance
    but strikes my life into some subsequent turning

Now out of the depth of sunken worlds you arise and kiss me
    and offer a bewitched apple to a throat aching
        which only tenderness can free

As I reach into the void which draws then and now apart
    ringing miraculously your voice returns and lingers

The gold-leaf foam-peonies dance a promise which becomes air
    and Nothing touches my fingers

After this painful resurrection I must sorrow again
   for my three lost loves which are you
      until the next burial, the next sleeping

And I know that all I have ever lost and will ever lose is you
   and the sea once more returns to her customary weeping

2. Epic

   Epics generally are heroic tales about cultural heroes or peoples. The <u>Ramayana</u> is an epic which tells the tale of the Indian hero, Rama.

EXAMPLE

The True and Tender Wife

[Rama, banished for fourteen years by his father, King Dasaratha, bids farewell to his wife, Sita, saying he must wander alone in the pathless woods. Sita, epitome of fidelity, answers.]

Rama spake, and soft-eyed Sita, ever sweet in speech and word,
Stirred by loving woman's passion boldly answered thus her lord:

"Do I hear my husband rightly, are these words my Rama spake,
And her banished lord and husband will the wedded wife forsake?

Lightly I dismiss the counsel which my lord hath lightly said,
For it ill beseems a warrior and my husband's princely grade!

*For the faithful woman follows where her wedded lord may lead,
In the banishment of Rama, Sita's exile is decreed.*

*Sire nor son nor loving brother rules the wedded woman's state,
With her lord she falls or rises, with her consort courts her
  fate.*

*If the righteous son of Raghu wends to forests dark and drear,
Sita steps before her husand wild and thorny paths to clear!*

Like the tasted refuse water cast thy timid thoughts aside,
Take me to the pathless jungle, bid me by my lord abide,

Car and steed and gilded palace vain are these to woman's life,
Dearer is her husband's shadow to the loved and loving wife!

For my mother often taught me and my father often spake
That her home the wedded woman doth beside her husband make,

As the shadow to the substance, to her lord is faithful wife,
And she parts not from her consort till she parts with fleet-
   ing life!

Therefore bid me seek the jungle and in pathless forests roam,
Where the wild deer freely ranges and the tiger makes his home,

Happier than in father's mansions in the woods will Sita rove,
Waste no thought on home or kindred, nestling in her husband's
   love!

World-renowned is Rama's valour, fearless by her Rama's side,
Sita will still live and wander with a faithful woman's pride,

And the wild fruit she will gather from the fresh and fragrant
   wood,
And the food by Rama tasted shall be Sita's cherished food!

Bid me seek the sylvan greenwoods, wooded hills and plateaus high,
Limpid rills and crystal *nullas* as they softly ripple by.

And when in the lake of lotus tuneful ducks their plumage lave,
Let me with my loving Rama skim the cool translucent wave!

Years will pass in happy union, -- happiest lot to woman given,--
Sita seeks not throne or empire, nor the brighter joys of heaven.

Heaven conceals not brighter mansions in its sunny fields of
   pride,
Where without her lord and husband faithful Sita would reside!

Therefore let me seek the jungle where the jungle-rangers rove,
Dearer than the royal palace where I share my husband's love,

And my heart in sweet communion shall my Rama's wishes share,
And my wifely toil shall lighten Rama's load of woe and care!"

Vainly gentle Rama pleaded dangers of the jungle life,
Vainly spake of toil and trial to a true and tender wife.

3. Dramatic

There are dramas written entirely in poetry form. Some narrative poetry also may be called dramatic in that it tells a story.

EXAMPLE

Radhadevi's Dance

[The Hammira-mahakavya or "Great Hammira Poem," is the work of a Jain monk. The excerpt tells of Radhadevi, King Hammira's favorite dancer, who dances on the battlefield just before she is slain by a traitor.]

In time the drummers beat their drums, the lutanists plucked
   their lutes,
the flautists blew their flutes.
Their voices in tune with the shrill flutes, the singers
sang the glory and fame of the brave Hammira....
Then, the vine of her body entrancing her lovers,
awakening passion with the glance of her half-closed eyes,
to delight the hearts of the courtiers,
came Radhadevi, the dancer arrayed for the dance.

The quivering buds of her fingers moved in the dance
like tendrils of a vine, thrilling with passion....
As the tips of her fingers bent, as though in a circle,
with her grace and delicate beauty all other girls seemed her
   slaves.
The moon, in the guise of the ring that trembled from the tip of
   her ear,
said: 'Your face is my likeness, the delusion even of sages!"
And as she danced she stirred the hearts of the young men watch-
   ing--
the hearts which lay like motes of camphor under her feet....
With her gestures the necklace trembled on the tip of her breasts
like a lotus twined in the beak of a swan.
When her body bent back like a bow in the dance
like a bowstring the braid of her hair stretched down to her
   heel....

And as she danced, at every beat of the rhythm,
she turned her back on the Saka king below.

Then in fury of soul the Lord of the Sakas spoke to his
   chamberlain:
'Is there any bowman who can make her his mark?'
His brother said: 'Sire, there is he whom you formerly threw
   into prison.
Uddanasimha -- he is the only man who can do it!'
At once the Saka king had him brought, and struck off his fetters,
and arrayed the traitor finely, with the double gift of affection.
And thus apparelled he took the bow which none but he could draw,
and the sinner shot her, as a hunter shoots a doe.

At the stroke of the arrow she fainted and fell in a moat,
as lightning falls from heaven.

Some Contemporary Forms of Poetry

1. Free Verse

Free verse has no specific rhyme scheme, rhythm, or beat. It therefore seems to be an easy form to compose. Actually, it is among the most difficult because of the freedom it seems to reveal. The imagists in the early part of the century used free verse with indications for a particular type of imagery it was to contain. This was known as objective imagery. "The leaves fall" was such an image. It is not a metaphor, yet contains evocative poetry.

EXAMPLE

I come from the dreary city

I come from the dreary city
to the reddish steaming plain,
to the blue foaming river
to cleanse myself
from the dust of the streets:
and as gleaming I emerge from the tides,
a cloud of golden bees draws near
and drapes itself like wings of fleece
about my shoulders:
and before me stands an Angel
who came on silver soles
wandering over, and speaks:
-- Have no fear: They do not sting.
They bring a honey message
from the blossoming tree
of Paradise.

(In the above poem, we also may note how the use of color enhances the mood and symbolism.)

2. The Prose Poem

The form is that of prose, but the imagery and the tone are those of poetry. Edgar Allan Poe, Stephane Mallarmé and Arthur Rimbaud were great innovators of the prose poem which recently has come into great favor among contemporary poets.

EXAMPLE

Farewell

AUTUMN ALREADY! -- But why regret an eternal sun if we are embarked on the discovery of divine light -- far from all those who die with the seasons.

Autumn. Risen through the motionless mists, our boat turns toward the port of misery, the enormous city with fire-and-mud-stained sky. Ah, the putrid rags, the rain-soaked bread, drunkenness, the thousand loves that have crucified me! Will she never have done, then, that ghoul queen of a million dead souls and dead bodies, *and that will be judged!* I see myself again, skin rotten with mud and pest, worms in my armpits and in my hair, and in my heart much bigger worms, lying among strangers without age, without feeling... I might have died there... Unbearable evocation! I loathe poverty.

And I dread winter because it is the season of comfort!

Sometimes in the sky I see endless beaches covered with white nations full of joy. Above me a great golden ship waves its multicolored pennants in the breezes of the morning. I created all possible festivities, all triumphs, all dramas. I tried to invent new flowers, new stars, new flesh, new tongues. I thought I was acquiring supernatural powers. Well! I must bury my imagination and my memories! An artist's and storyteller's precious fame flung away!

I! I who called myself angel or seer, exempt from all morality, I am returned to the soil with a duty to seek and rough reality to embrace! Peasant!

Am I mistaken? Would charity be the sister of death for me?

At last, I shall ask forgiveness for having fed on lies. And now let's go.

But no friendly hand! And where to turn for help!

YES, THE NEW HOUR is hard enough.

For I can say that victory is won: the gnashing of teeth, the hissings of fire, the pestilential sighs are abating. All the noisome memories are fading. My last regrets take to their heels, -- envy of beggars, thieves, of death's friends, of the backward of all kinds. O damned ones, what if I avenged myself!

One must be absolutely modern.

No hymns! Hold the ground gained. Arduous night! The dried blood smokes on my face, and I have nothing behind me but that horrible bush! . . . Spiritual combat is as brutal as the battle of men: but the vision of justice is the pleasure of God alone.

This, however, is the vigil. Welcome then, all the influx of vigor and real tenderness. And, in the dawn, armed with an ardent patience, we shall enter magnificent cities.

Why talk of a friendly hand! It's all to my advantage that I can laugh at old lying loves and put to shame those deceitful couples, -- I saw the hell of women back there; -- and I shall be free to *possess truth in one soul and one body.*

3. The Concrete Poem

This is known also as the <u>ideogram</u>: Through the placement of the words on the page, a picture is formed containing the image of the poem itself so that there is a multiple experience. The danger lies in the possibility that this may deteriorate into a materialistic game. This form is believed to be very "modern," but it originated in the Middle Ages when the image on the page became a symbol connected with religion: the Cross, the Altar, and the tomb were frequently represented. It was the surrealist poet, Apollinaire who used this form ingeniously to depict ordinary experiences, such as the arrangement into verse of a tear, rain falling, or a cravate.

EXAMPLES

"A New Poem by Daisy Aldan"

Outside an artfully defined
ZerO, under a full mOOn, Virgo's sign,
Your deftly carved NOthing loomed
In a clear azure Absolute.
Designed NO-memories skirted the rounding
Bonds which yet wound us about
And sinuously snaked, and consumed
Us inside a NAUGHT that strangled
But you slipped skillfully out
Of our mutual nOOse, and cruelly dangled
Friendship in a hollow of loss.
Circles swallowed your eyes whose
Denial now doomed the whirling abyss
Unfurling a giant who rose
From the core of the coil, steered
Toward the sun by a mercury star

ALONE
LONE
ONE

Thus I freed you from the steely glow of my need

Where I had burnt incense and made blood sacrifices.

The English Hunter

Tossing her mane from her eyes she has become like the animal she so adores, the thorough bred filly. Her head high, she canters with pride. Yells seems to glow as she falls into moods, either vibrant and she has all know about it as to her own ideas and uncomfortable, and she has letting all know about it as she resists her position. She is frightened and wears her complaint across her face. Like a horse, she grunts and grumbles with her discomfort. She knows no patience with those who annoy her. Wild, the thoroughbred resists authority, wishing none to restrain her. Her stance is long-legged and slender. Her shoes are like hoofs supporting her fine form. My eye lids silently close and I caress her racing, un- tamed free. doing what her heart pleases. mal she loves with the ani- decided to devote she has life to its care breeding. For her, the thoroughbred is what she is.

Her coat, always immaculate, when her apparel accidentally is soiled. She is hard to break, stubbornly adhering standards. At times she cruelly subdued or alive ed she becomes when mastered the skill of she whines and resists of loud noises across

105

4. "To Let the Light in"

The poem on this page which seems to be but is neither an ideogram nor a picture uses spacing in a creative way, "to let the light in," as Mallarmé stated.

EXAMPLE

In Fog

in heavy warm fog thick

      with   nimbus

               nets

          the   Dead

     weave   rainbow

haloes

                              among ghosts of

                                    lightless

                                    leaves

Remember, the possibilities of form in contemporary poetry are infinite and depend only upon the artistry and ingenuity of the poet himself. Although exquisite classical poems have come down to us as a heritage, contemporary poetry is also filled with richness. However, the very freedom allowed has also given birth to distortions, obscenities, and horrors which find their way into publication. Each writer must assume a sense of responsibility for the work he presents to the world. Judgment, taste, and discrimination must be developed hand in hand with the craft.

Exercises

1. Attempt a poem in each of the classical forms. Such exercises are invaluable for developing attention to words, sounds, omissions, etc.

2. Write a poem in free verse. Or transform the above classical poems into free verse. Note how tone alters.

3. Write a prose poem on a chosen theme.

4. Try some ideograms. These are most enjoyable exercises and help to develop discipline and choice.

5. Write a poem which uses exaggerated spacing and unusual typography.

6. Now is the time you must pay careful attention to stanza structure, making patterns of couplets, tercets, etc.

Metre and Rhythm

Metre often distinguishes poetry from prose. It is measured beat. The English language which was influenced by the rhythm of waters does not lend itself to regular beats as does the Greek or German, and yet, even in English, one may desire to use defined metrical patterns to express particular experiences.

It is from ancient Greece that we derive the metres most of us know. The Greek poets knew how certain arrangements of sound could speak to the heart and influence behavior. Many so-called primitive peoples know this also, and in certain tribes defined beats are used as magic to influence men and gods. In our own Western environment, we see how, in a debased fashion, this technique of persuasion is used in commercials by television agencies.

Metre is a measurable beat; rhythm on the other hand, has to do with the "music" of poetry -- the inner flow, the intangible.

The "music" of poetry is different from that which is created by musical instruments. It may be heard by the inner ear even when one reads poetry silently.

Metres are measured by long and short syllables, stressed and unstressed syllables which are indicated thus:

$\smile$ short

$-$ long

There are many metres. Those most widely known are:

1. Iambic: ∪ —— Short **Long**

The iambic originated from the *Jambe*, a divinity of the Mysteries of Eleusis. It is connected with the diastole systole of the heartbeat, and certain verses were spoken to an iambic beat in order to draw forth particular reactions from the assembly. The iambic encourages the feeling of strong egohood, will-force, strength, a forward direction, determination. Marching soldiers often respond to the iambic:

   Hup ONE! Hup TWO! Hup THREE! Hup FOUR!

   It is easy to remember because the first two syllables seem to say, I AM!

   Many classic writers used the iambic in poetic drama. Shakespeare used <u>blank verse</u> a good deal, and this is in <u>iambic pentameter</u>, or five beats to a line.

   As it happens, the iambic is one of the few metres to which the English language lends itself. Example: To<u>day</u> I <u>met</u> a <u>wo</u>man <u>in</u> the <u>park</u>.

Exercise

   Write out any line in iambic metre.

   Clap out the metre with your hands.

   Walk around the room to the beat of short <u>long</u>/ short <u>long</u>/ short <u>long</u>.

2. Trochaic: —— ∪ **Long Short**

   The trochaic expresses a thoughtful, serious or sad mood. It was used at the Mysteries of Eleusis when the faithful there entered the inner temple. The use of different beats is able to change the very heartbeat and breathstream, and thus transformation of consciousness may be brought about. Example: <u>All</u> our <u>pride</u> is <u>but</u> a <u>jest</u>...

Exercise

   Write a line using trochaic metre.

   Clap out this metre with your hands.

   Walk around the room to the trochaic beat: <u>long</u> short / <u>long</u> short/ <u>long</u> short.

   Put into words the difference you feel when walking to the iambic and the trochaic.

3. Anapest: ∪ ∪ —— Short Short <u>Long</u>

The anapest is often used in narrative poetry. The attention is focused on the long or stressed syllable. In reading poetry, particularly aloud, clarity is enhanced if one recognizes the beat. Confusion results if one stresses the wrong syllables. Inexperienced readers often do this and a sing-songy effect and meaningless reading result. Example: "It was <u>many</u> and <u>many</u> a <u>year</u> <u>ago</u>..."

Here we have a combination of the anapest and the iambic. Edgar Allan Poe was a genius of metre and often varied beats, making ingenious combinations.

Exercise

Write a line in anapest metre. Clap out the beats. Walk around the room to the anapest metre: short short <u>long</u> / short short <u>long</u> / short short <u>long</u>.

It is interesting to note that many people are unable to do this properly at first. This shows some lack of balance, and may be corrected by the practice of this exercise. So we realize the power of regulated beats and their connection with the whole human being.

4. Dactyl: —— ∪ ∪ <u>Long</u> Short Short

The dactyl is very dynamic and may be likened to horses' hoofbeats. Example: <u>Half</u> a league, <u>half</u> a league, ...

Exercise

Write a line in dactylic metre. Clap out the beat. Walk around the room to the beat of the dactyl: <u>long</u> short short / <u>long</u> short short / <u>long</u> short short.

Put into words the difference you feel when doing the anapest and dactyl.

5. Spondee: —— —— <u>Long Long</u>

The spondee is used for interjections, emphasis, strength. Example: Hark!Hark! Help!Help! Here!Now!

Exercise

Write a line using the spondee. Clap out the spondee. Walk around the room to the spondee: <u>Long</u> <u>Long</u> / <u>Long</u> <u>Long</u> / <u>Long</u> <u>Long</u>. What is the mood you experience in the spondee?

More Exercises

1. Indicate and analyze the metres of particular poems. Note the tone (mood) of the poem.

2. Write a poem on some aspect of our theme, Tides, and create a definite metrical pattern.

3. Indicate the metres by the signs for short long.

4. Name the metres you have used.

This is an excellent discipline and will train you in condensation, choice and omission. The serious student who really wishes to master the art of poetry will not be satisfied to do one exercise, but will give himself assignments according to the indications in this book. As a pianist would never learn to play serious compositions without the discipline of daily exercises, so the writer, no matter how talented he may be, will never become a master without daily disciplined exercises.

Scansion

Scansion is the arrangement and disposition of metre, or the measuring of verse by what is known as <u>poetic feet</u>.

Lines may be of different lengths and a different number of verse feet. When structuring a poem, one may arrange the lines and verse feet in the pattern which best expresses what the poet wishes to communicate. This is known as <u>composition</u>.

For example, an arrangement may be made thus:

```
U U — U U — U U — U —
U U — U — U —
U U — U — U U — U —
U U — U — U U —
U U — U U — U — U U —
U U — U U — U —

— U U — U — U U —
U U — U — U —
U U — U U — U U — U —
— U U — U U —
U U — U U — U — U U —
— U U — U —
```

It was many and many a year ago
In a kingdom by the sea
That a maiden there lived whom you may know
By the name of Annabel Lee,
And this maiden she lived with no other thought
Than to love and be loved by me.

I was a child and she was a child
In this kingdom by the sea
But we loved with a love that was more than love,
I and my Annabel Lee;
With a love that the winged seraphs of heaven
Coveted her and me...

Verse Feet

The measure of a verse is determined by the number of feet in a line.

Monometer: A line using one verse foot:

Dimeter: A line using two verse feet:
U — U —

Trimeter: A line using three verse feet:
U — U — U —

Tetrameter: Four verse feet:
U — U — U — U —

Pentameter: Five verse feet:
U — U — U — U — U —

Hexameter: Six verse feet:
U — U — U — U — U — U —

Heptameter: Seven verse feet:
U — U — U — U — U — U — U —

Octometer: Eight verse feet:
U — U — U — U — U — U — U — U —

Examples of Verse Feet

<u>Monometer</u>

The winds
Pass by;
The birds
Fly.

<u>Dimeter</u>

Birds wings/are spread

<u>Trimeter</u>

The night/was dark/and dreary

<u>Tetrameter</u>

It was man/y and man/y a year/ ago

<u>Pentameter</u>

The trees/were bare/against/ a lead/en sky

<u>Hexameter</u>

This is the/forest prim/eval. The/murmuring/pines and the/hemlocks

<u>Heptameter or Septenary</u>

More love/ly and/more joy/ful than/the danc/ing waves/reveal/

Evaluating the Poem

The developing poet should acquire the habit of evaluating his own poems as well as the poetry of others. Skill and experience in detecting flaws, tuning of the inner ear, and the enlarging of vision may be developed.

Here are some questions to ask concerning the poem:

1. What is the <u>intention</u> of this poem?

2. What is the central unifying <u>tone</u>? Is the tone carried through, or might confusion <u>arise</u>?

3. What <u>images</u> have I used? Are there cliches? Is there unity? Have I intentionally or unintentionally mixed metaphors?

4. For the sake of clarity and artistry, is there anything I may still omit? Ruthlessness is called for here.

5. Is my <u>structure</u> suitable to and inherent in all aspects of the <u>poem</u>? Is my <u>spacing</u> integral, or simply haphazard?

6. Has my <u>sound structure</u> enhanced the poem's mood and meaning? Are my <u>rhymes</u> interesting, forced, obvious?

7. Is there a special <u>idea</u> I desired to convey? What is it? Is it clear or <u>obscure</u>? It is not implied that the poem must be simplified to reach a mediocre reader -- an intelligent attentive reader is assumed. Rather, one's attitude should be to enlarge the experience of the reader and to raise his level of understanding through the poem.

8. Finally, one must ask oneself: Is this poem worthy of being brought out into the world? Will it enhance the experience of even one reader? If the answer is yes, then you are on the way toward being worthy of the title, Poet.

"...The poet is not the coldly bored observer, or the enemy of, the sneerer of, his readers. He is a brother speaking to a brother of 'a moment of their other lives' -- a moment that had been buried beneath the dust of the busy world...The poet is the complete lover of mankind..."

       Edith Sitwell

Preparing for Publication

Many people who begin to write poetry immediately desire to see their names in print. Do not be in a rush to have your work published before it is ready, or you will waste time, effort, and money. You should have a substantial amount of worthy work before you begin to send poems to publishers. Objective judgment is essential for anyone meriting the name of artist. When the time is ripe for publication, it is important to know how the manuscript should be prepared, what periodicals exist, which literary organizations one should approach, and which publishers may be interested in poetry manuscripts, among other things.

To write poetry for one's own enjoyment is one thing, but to be a poet in the world is an entirely different situation.

The Manuscript

Poems should be typed neatly on standard size typing paper.

Some publications will accept only original copies: However, in recent years, good photocopies are acceptable.

Never send carbon copies.

Number the pages.

Unless single space is essential to the tone and structure of the poem, use double space.

Make sure there are no errors in spelling, grammar, or punctuation.

Place your name low and to the right of the manuscript.

If your poem is returned, do not send out that copy again unless it is thoroughly neat.

Include a self-addressed stamped envelope. This is often indicated in requests for material as SASE.

Include a brief accompanying letter with brief biographical notes. Never write a long personal letter with your woes and opinions. If someone has suggested you to the editor, mention that.

Send from four to six poems.

If you are planning to make money from the publication of your poetry, you are living in an illusion. Very rarely does a good poet earn even a minimum amount of money. Rather, the year's end will more frequently show a loss, in terms of cost of mailings, etc. This is the nature of the poetry situation in our time. Try to begin to consider your poetry as a free gift to the world. Few publications pay for poems. Usually you will receive two copies of the magazine in which your work appears.

Some Pertinent Publications

International Directory of Little Magazines and Small Presses. Dustbooks, P. O. Box 100, Paradise, CA 93969.

Directory of Small Magazine Press Editors and Publishers. Dustbooks, See above.

Guide to Women's Publishing, Andrea Chesman and Polly Joan. Women's Writing Press, R. D. 3, Newfield, N.Y. 14867.

The Publish-It-Yourself Handbook, ed. Bill Henderson. Pushcart Press, Box 845, Yonkers, N.Y. 10701.

The Little Magazine in America: A Documentary History. ed. Elliot Anderson and Mary Kinzie. Pushcart Press, See above.

Publications from Poets and Writers. 204 West 54 Street, N.Y.C. 10019.

Coda: Poets and Writers Newsletter

A Writer's Guide to Copyright

Sponsor's List

A Directory of American Poets and Fiction Writers

Literary Agents: A Complete Guide

Literary Bookstores in the U.S.

Grants and Awards. American P.E.N. 47 Fifth Avenue, N.Y.C. 10003

    The above will get you started. A wealth of further material may be found in the public libraries and in literary book stores.

    Make it a habit to read the volumes of good published poetry. Most libraries have subscriptions to literary periodicals. Make yourself familiar with those. University libraries often have outstanding collections of poetry and literary periodicals. Read poetry of the past of all nations. In our time, many good translations exist and these are sources of knowledge and inspiration. Get to know the literary bookstores in your area and make contact with them. Often they hold or can be convinced to hold poetry readings.

Some Poetry Organizations to Consider

American P.E.N., 47 Fifth Avenue, N.Y.C. 10003.
You must be recommended and have at least two published books to your credit.

The Poetry Society of America, 15 Gramercy Park, N.Y.C. 10010.
A specific number of poems must be submitted for consideration by the executive board. Known authors are accepted on the basis of reputation and accomplishment.

Poets and Writers, 201 West 54 Street, N.Y.C. 10019.
Requirements for listing may be obtained by writing to the organization.

Academy of American Poetry, 177 East 87 Street, N.Y.C. 10028.
Not a strict membership organization, but a sponsor of numerous poetry activities and awards. Their bulletin *Pilot* has much material of interest to poets.

    In addition, regional poetry organizations and clubs exist all over the United States of America. The above organizations may be contacted for the addresses of those in your area.

The Poem

The Poem Is:
I gather the poem from The Poem.
I listen to the butterfly-wing-whir of the poem
which I make into a temple for The Poem.
I am the poem,
the temple of The Poem.

The poem is a beehive.
the poem is a flower,
as I am a beehive,
as I am a flower.
as I am a string of seashells.

It is the sand image fashioned by wind-wails
or sea-sound-whirls;
a footstep, - unique as each living leaf:
It is the face my mind carves in a mountain,
or the aquarelle of an ancient in a lake-swirl.

Someone dances the poem,
someone sings the poem:
I send the poem to love someone;
the poem is an embrace:
The poem can revenge,
the poem can kill:
Someone cries out,
another weeps.
I heal with the poem.
I make someone laugh:
The poem rocks one to sleep:
Someone dreams the poem.

The poem is apex where past and future encounter.
The poem gives birth to the poem:
The poem is the child I conceive with The Poem:
this child is my Self.

The poem is equation of Light/light!

                            Daisy Aldan

Index to Authors and Poems

ALDAN, Daisy: Ambiguous connection, 14; A New Poem, 104; "B", 68; Contemplations: the lake, 37; Flight, 16; In a perpetual dusk, 65; In fog, 106; In the winter city, 39; The Little Mermaid, 13; mercurial pitching sunbeams, 82; Out of her exile, 79; out of the sleeping deep, 97; The Poem, 120; Portrait of W.M., 49; Seven Dreams Appear, 40; Song: leave, say never, 16; *from* Spring, 72; Tides, 21; The Wave, 84; Word play: Washington Square, 70.

Anonymous, The Douglas Tragedy, 104
ASHBERY, John: A Pastoral, 95.
BARRETT, Susan E.; *from* the sea, 31.
BENSON, Linda: Soul moods, 59-60.
BRETON, Andre: Curtain Curtain (trans. by D. Aldan), 41.
BROOKE, Ruppert: *from* The Great Lover, 55.
BROWNING, Robert: *from* My Last Duchess, 74.
BYRON, Lord: *from* Don Juan, 87.
CARROLL, Lewis: Jabberwocky, 69.
CHI HA, Kim: Blue Clothes, 64; By the Sea, 51.
COHEN, Diana: Dissolving Beach, 51.
CREELEY, Robert: If You, 85.
DICKINSON, Emily: Love's stricken "Why", 72; The grass divides, 73.
DRYDEN, John: *from* Alexander's Feast, 25.
ELIOT, Thomas Stearns: *from* the Love Song of J. Alfred Prufrock, 26.
FIELD, Edward: Donkeys, 47.
GOLDBERG, Phylis: Seduction, 28.
GOULD, Roberta: Living Space, 26.
GRILIKHES, Alexandra: Aphrodite, her birth, 60.
HANSON, Pauline: Clouds, 63.
HENLEY, W.B.: *from* What is to come 74; Rondeau, 91.
HERRICK, Robert: Upon Julia's Clothes, 86.
HOPKINS, Gerard Manley: *from* the Windhover, 72, 75.
JEFFERSON, Kieth: *from* Anatomy of Prayer, 61.
KAUFMAN, Rochelle: Thoroughbred, 105.
KEATS, John: *from* the Eve of St. Agnes, 88.
KILMER, Joyce: *from* Trees, 72.
LORCA, Frederico Garcia: The Ballad of the Water of the Sea (trans by D. Aldan), 32.

MALLARMÉ, Stephane: *from* a Throw of the Dice (trans. by D. Aldan), 81.
MEREDITH, William: In the Rif Mountains, 29.
MORITAKE: Haiku, 96.
MORGENSTERN, Christian: The great Lalula, 70.
MORRISON, Lillian: The Ghosts of Jersey City, 38.
MURRAY, Paul D.: The Barn on Seven Star Road, 12; The Mute, 47.
O'HARA: Ode to Willem De Kooning, 92.
PENNANT, Edmund: The Pleiades, 13.
POE, Edgar Allan: *from* Annabel Lee, 112.
RIMBAUD, Arthur: Farewell *from* A Season in Hell, 102.
ROSETTI, Christian: *from* Rest, 74; The Bourne, 86.
ROSETTI, Dante Gabriel: *from* The Blessed Damozel, 87.
SCHECHTER, Ruth Lisa: Translations from the Russian, 33.
SHAKESPEARE, William: *from* Hamlet, 30; *from* King Lear, 31; *from* Love's Labour Lost, 77; *from* Richard II, 30; Sonnet XXIX, 89; *from* The Tempest, 30.
SHELLEY, Percy B.: *from* Ode to the West Wind, 25.
SITWELL, Edith: *from* Sir Beelzebub, 73; Still falls the rain, 73.
SPENSER, Sylvia: White Weather, 82.
STEFFEN, Albert: I come from the dreary city (trans. by D. Aldan), 101; *from* The Death Experience of Manes (trans. by D. Aldan), 96.
STEINER, Rudolf: Mantram, 17.
STOREY, Francine: Instructions for search, 27.
SURI NAYACANDRA: *from* Radhadevi's Dance (from the Hammira Mahakavya), 100.
SWINBURNE, Charles Alergnon, A Ballad of Dreamland, 90. A Leave-Taking, 105.
TAGORE, Rabindranath: On the Seashore, 35.
TENNYSON, Alfred L.: Blow Bugle Blow, 74.
THOMAS, Dylan: Do not go gentle, 91.
VALMIKI: The True and Tender Wife (from the Ramayana), 98.
ZINNES, Harriet: *from* Fear, 24; Relic, 76.
WHITMAN, Walt: *from* Song of the Rolling Earth, 2.

LIBRARY OF DAVIDSON COLLEGE